# School Tools

## Structures for Learning

# School Tools

## Structures for Learning

Eric S. Elkins

**fulcrum resources**
Golden, Colorado

Library of Congress Cataloging-in-Publication Data

Elkins, Eric S.
        School tools : structures for learning / Eric S.
Elkins.
            p.      cm.
        Includes index.
        ISBN 1-55591-974-X (pbk. : alk. paper)
        1. Learning.  2. Teaching.  I. Title.
LB1060.E445   1999
370.15'23—dc21                                    99–34306
                                                  CIP


Printed in the United States of America
        0 9 8 7 6 5 4 3 2 1

Cover image by Joshua C. Barchers
Cover design by Deborah Rich

Fulcrum Publishing
350 Indiana Street, Suite 350
Golden, Colorado 80401-5093
(800) 992-2908 • (303) 277-1623
www.fulcrum-resources.com

# Permissions Acknowledgments

I truly appreciate the permission granted by the following organizations to refer lesson plans in this book to the National Standards that they developed.

National Council of Teachers of English
1111 W. Kenyon Road
Urbana, IL 61801-1096

*Standards for the English Language Arts*, by the International Reading Association and National Council of Teachers of English, Copyright ©1996 by the International Reading Association and National Council of Teachers of English. Reprinted with permission.

National Geographic Society
1145 17th Street NW.
Washington, DC 20036-4688

National Academy of Sciences
2101 Constitution Avenue NW
Washington, DC 20418

*National Science Education Standards*,
National Committee on Science Education Standards and Assessment, National Research Council, 1996

National Center for History in the Schools
UCLA, Department of History
405 Hilgard Avenue
Los Angeles, CA 90024-1473

National Standards for United States History, World History, and K–4 History

National Council for the Social Studies
3501 Newark Street, NW
Washington, DC 20016

*My heartfelt appreciation and admiration go out to
the teachers whose efforts made this book possible.*

*Bill, Peter, Kathy, Kim, Linda, Jim, Jerry, Doug, Dad, and Mom,
I cannot thank you sufficiently.*

*This book is dedicated to my favorite teacher, Jennifer.*

# Contents

# Foreword
## by Bill Juraschek

Have you ever watched an ice sculptor at work? Before your eyes this artisan deftly chips, scrapes, picks, and torches an unremarkable block of ice into a praying angel, a growling tiger, whatever they visualize. The eventual raves of the viewers attest to the sculptor's skill with basic tools: chisels, ice picks, and a blow torch. If we think of carving the ice into a work of art as a problem to solve, then the sculptor solves his or her problem through skillful use of basic tools, not unlike anyone who is trying to solve a problem.

Recent school reform efforts have called for emphasis on problem solving, that is, helping students learn what to do when they want to reach a goal but no path is apparent. What the problem-solving advocates have not sufficiently emphasized is the fact that no one, just like an ice sculptor, can solve a problem unless he or she has command of the necessary tools. Also, much of the call for problem-solving instruction has come from the mathematics community, but any thoughtful teacher wants to help students become problem solvers across the curriculum. Students encounter problems in science, social studies, language arts, technology, and so on. Indeed, for too many students, succeeding in school is problematical. Mastering a set of tools that are useful for solving problems in all areas of learning is the idea behind *School Tools*.

Incorporating a combination of contemporary and traditional pedagogy, this collection of classroom–tested activities focuses on seven "tools" that are basic for success across the curriculum of the middle grades and beyond. Although the units focus on a particular area, such as writing within selected structures, they also contain many connections to other areas. The units are fairly prescriptive at first, but quickly encourage students to become independent, a practice known as "scaffolding."

*School Tools* began as Eric's project in a graduate course on problem solving. As he tried the activities in his classroom and became more convinced of the soundness of the tools— first pedagogy, he expanded the project into his final master's project and, ultimately, this book. *School Tools* is a welcome example of what a creative teacher can do with a good idea. I feel certain you will also find this pedagogy effective.

Bill Juraschek
University of Colorado at Denver

# Introduction

## Rationale for the *School Tools* Unit

So often, with the endlessly evolving curriculum in every district, the requirements of standards, and additional responsibilities placed on the classroom teacher, we find ourselves overwhelmed with the need to "cover" content material. By diving headlong into the curriculum and spouting out information at a break-neck pace, teachers may not give the students a chance to digest new information. Sometimes students don't even have a mental framework into which they can accommodate the information they are required (by the teacher, district, or state) to know. In this *School Tools* unit, students forgo the specifics of some content areas for a brief time (three weeks or so) to develop and practice using a "box of tools," or set of strategies, which will provide structure for future learning. By putting aside grade-specific content to help students get used to using these tools, the teacher, in the long run, will save time, energy, and the heartache of hit-or-miss instruction.

Fortunately, there is no need to abandon content standards to run this unit. Every lesson is standards referenced with the relevant national content standards. Thus, even when a teacher sets aside a few weeks to teach *School Tools*, he or she will be addressing the standards. This unit introduces the needed background for future student attainment of these standards. In other words, although the teacher will be assessing abilities based on the standards addressed, most students will need more than this three-week unit to become proficient.

Because students often need repetition of routine procedures to make certain behaviors into habit, all the tools in this unit must be used again and again. The more students practice these strategies, the more often and fluently they will be able to apply them to content. As we tested this unit, we saw a steady increase in ability and frequency of use over time. Several months later, students naturally tended to speak of cause and effect when discussing events, were comfortable and consistent with the scientific process, and were writing well-organized essays.

It may help to look at the overall process of developing the School Tools. These phases are:

Introduction
Guided Practice
Exercise
Application
Risk

Allow students to become habituated to using the tools instinctively and without struggle. You will provide direct instruction in the Introduction phase of the process. Next you will assist students in Guided Practice. Exercise, in which the students work independently, but still somewhat out of context of the true, long-term use of the tools, is at the heart of this unit. The Application phase of the process comes when you head back into content, but still require the students to use the School Tools on a daily basis. Finally, students who manage to use the tools proficiently and fluently naturally slip into the Risk phase, where they work beyond the basic scope of the tools, modifying them and applying them for their own needs. The phase designation of each lesson is provided within the lesson plans.

# How to Use This Unit

The best time to use this unit is at the beginning of the school year. By learning expectations of format and procedure early on, students will rapidly become habituated to those norms. *School Tools* is designed to be a three-week unit, but more or less time can be given, depending on the needs of the students. We ended up stretching the *School Tools* lessons into our content areas and didn't bring closure to the unit until six weeks into the year.

If the thought of using this book as a replacement unit is daunting, each chapter can also work as a single area of focus. In other words, because the chapters are centered around specific, related tools, the teacher could pick a chapter, use it alone until students are competent with its tools, then move on to another chapter. So, instead of looking at this book as a three- or four-week unit unto itself (except, of course, the mid-term and end-of-year chapters), each chapter can be used as a single mini-unit.

The lessons are broken down into several areas: Newspaper, Math/Geography, Social Studies/Language Arts, Science, and Language Arts. An attempt has been made to integrate the tools across the curriculum. Thus, the recognition of cause and effect relationships is encouraged in all areas. Although the lessons are presented in the order in which we used them, each teacher will certainly find the most viable sequence for his or her classroom. All lessons should be used for assessment purposes, to check student levels and progress, but closure assessments are also provided.

By setting aside three weeks to concentrate solely on these tools, the teacher should see an improvement in the ability of students to interpret new information. The tools in this unit will provide a mental organizer for student thought, a system for the integration of ideas and concepts.

Many additional activities are provided, far more than could be executed in the unit's time. These lessons are to be used to maintain and enhance skills throughout the school year. As you read through them, decide which you will use every week and which will work as review about halfway through the school year.

Finally, two chapters are dedicated to review and assessment. First, the mid-term review unit (Chapter 6) provides ample opportunity to renew expectations, review student use of School Tools, and remind students of their use. The final chapter, designed for the last weeks of school, allows students and teachers to look back over the school year, evaluate how the School Tools were used, and prepare for their application beyond the current range of study.

You will know best what your students need and how they will respond to the lessons in this book. Therefore, all lessons are written to be adaptable and flexible. Extension and modification ideas are included with every lesson. If you page through each lesson before implementing the unit, you will be able to decide which lessons will work for you and which are expendable.

# Unit Overview

## Tools to Develop

### Writing Process

Students use a highly prescriptive framework for composing nonfiction and fiction works. Once they have mastered these specific structures, they will be able to elaborate creatively on each format.

### How to Read a Newspaper

As a public document, the newspaper is a constantly changing tool that students can use in all content areas. By introducing them to some of its uses and structures, the teacher will prime students for future newspaper exploits during the school year.

### Multiplication Math Facts

Included in this chapter are organizers for helping students improve their math facts competence.

### Awareness of Cause and Effect Relationships

This skill will provide a useful perspective for students. By interpreting events (historical, scientific, and social) through the lens of cause and effect, students become accustomed to organizing their schema into a logical structure.

### Scientific Observation/Method

Students become conversant with the scientific inquiry process through practice. Their assumptions about what they observe are also challenged to focus their data collection on what can be proven or measured.

### Using a Map

Reading the scale and understanding longitude and latitude coordinates prove useful in student research.

### Writing a Problem–Solving Report

Students learn to document their problem-solving process, to share their comprehension.

# School Tools

## Structures for Learning

## Chapter 1
# Language Arts Lessons

## Introduction

The language arts lessons in this chapter dwell on three specific School Tools. The first is the development of common language and structures for organized written expression. Next, editing skills, through practice and discussion, are necessary as students proofread their own work and that of their peers. In the reading section of this chapter, students focus on cause and effect relationships in the novels they read.

## Developing Language
## and Formats for Organized Writing

There is nothing worse than trying to grade a student's 10-page, handwritten tome, which either starts with the student waking up and carefully describes every painful detail of the student's day, or is a terribly mixed up (and often derivative) attempt at a fictional story. Although I have nothing against Nintendo 64 (hey, I own one myself), long-winded play-by-plays about a road race between MarioCart characters do not make for very exciting reading.

The following lessons are prescriptive, but they help students to learn the process of organized written expression. Students learn to write paragraphs, essays, and stories in concrete formats that make their writing easier to read, tend to stay on topic, and are easier to compose (once they get the processes down). Although students may chafe at the strict formats at first, they will gradually see the benefits to writing this way.

After individual students show proficiency with each format, you may decide to let them play with the arrangement of sentences and paragraphs to fit their personal styles. I always tell my students that they need to learn the basic writing structures first. Knowing the formats and the rules is essential before they can be broken in an effective manner. I also let students know that these writing processes will be useful for the rest of their lives. (Explaining that they'll be writing paragraphs and essays for the rest of their school careers, at least, often helps motivate my students to learn this stuff.)

First, students learn how to write a simple, yet well-formed, paragraph. They watch as the teacher models the process, from brainstorming through writing a quick outline to creating a focused work. Once students have had plenty of practice, the next logical step is to learn how to write an essay.

The essay format is not too complicated, but it allows students to understand the structure very quickly. Although the step-by-step lesson takes several days, students tend to learn the pattern quickly. Again, quite a bit of practice is also involved, to help the students truly understand how to plan and write an organized essay. Later in the school year, when students show a consistent ability to write organized essays, you may wish to expand their writing toolbox into other forms of written expression.

Writing a fiction story can be very complicated without proper planning. Although the story format is very simplistic, it allows students to think through their entire oeuvres without too much trouble. As students learn the basic structure, they can modify and extend it.

Students who are proficient in the essay format will truly enjoy writing persuasive essays. Although you may wish to start out by giving them topics to discuss, students become quite eager to write cogent discourses of their own (sometimes inexplicable) opinions.

These lessons barely touch on the mechanics of written work. Unless the writing contains so many errors that it is incomprehensible, focus on helping the students understand the structures when teaching these formats. Although I would not say spelling and punctuation are not important, I would push formats first and foremost in these lessons!

## Editing Practice

For students to be able to edit their work and the work of their peers, they need practice. Use these worksheets periodically to help students recognize when errors occur. These sheets have been created in different formats to help students practice editing under various conditions.

## Novels

Recognizing cause and effect relationships in reading is a great way for students to monitor their comprehension. They can trace important events in the book to earlier causes or can predict future effects of events as they read them. In the math section of this book, students also track the journeys characters take.

# A Well-Formed Paragraph

**Purpose:**  To introduce a process for writing in paragraph form.

**Process:**  Students are taught how to plan and write a single, focused paragraph.

**Payoff:**  This is the first step in a process that will lead to writing an entire essay or story.

**Phases:**  Introduction, Guided Practice

## Standards Addressed

### *English Language Arts*

4. Students adjust their use of spoken, written, and visual language (e.g., conventions, style, vocabulary) to communicate effectively with a variety of audiences for a variety of purposes.

5. Students apply knowledge of language structure, language conventions (e.g., spelling and punctuation), media techniques, figurative language, and genre to create, critique, and discuss print and nonprint texts.

12. Students use spoken, written, and visual language to accomplish their own purposes (e.g., for learning, enjoyment, persuasion, and the exchange of information).

## Materials Needed

**Students Need:**  Notebook paper, pencils

**Teacher Needs:**  Overhead projector, blank transparencies, several colors of overhead markers

## Steps

1. Ask students to explain what they know about paragraphs. Lead a discussion on the form, function, and purpose of writing in paragraph form. Be sure important aspects such as indenting and skipping a line between paragraphs are mentioned. A paragraph is written about a single subject or event. It focuses only on that subject. A paragraph helps the reader better understand what is written because it is organized.

2. To model the planning and writing of a paragraph, start by explaining that you will be writing a paragraph about a single event that occurred to you over the previous weekend (or vacation).

3. On the transparency, start out by writing "Brainstorm." The first step is to make a list of different things that you did over the weekend. Write down four or five things (make them entertaining; although your students may not want to hear how you washed your hair, the difficulties in washing the cat may keep their interest!). Go through the list with the class and choose a single subject to pursue.

4. On the same transparency sheet, write down the chosen topic of your paragraph. Under it, write down five or six things that would support or describe the event you are using. Narrow down your list to three key points by crossing out things that are interesting but not important (or, of course, neither interesting nor important).

5. Have students complete the same exercise. They need to brainstorm several activities from the weekend, then pick one. Next, they need to brainstorm supporting details and circle only three.

6. On the transparency, explain that you need to create a "topic sentence" for your paragraph. A topic sentence tells what the paragraph is about. Supporting sentences add details to support the topic. Next to your chosen topic, write a phrase that turns your subject into a complete sentence. Put a capital Roman numeral one (I) before your topic sentence and capital letters in front of the supporting details in the order in which you will write about them. You may write each letter in a different color to correspond with the sentences as you write them in your paragraph.

> I. Colby—I spent some time with my buddy Colby over the weekend.
>      always tells bad jokes
>      B. talked about books
>      A. played video games
>      C. ate pizza
>      vegetarian
>      wives went shoe shopping

7. Have students write a topic sentence and fill in the outline around their notes.

8. On a new transparency, begin to write your paragraph. Have your outline visible at the top of the screen and show the students how you follow it. Explain that you indented the topic sentence and how you turned your supporting ideas into complete sentences.

> I spent some time with my buddy, Colby, over the weekend. Most of the time, we played video games at my house. We also talked about the books we're reading right now. When we got hungry, we ordered a large pizza and split it.

9. Simple, yet effective, isn't it? Have your students write their own paragraphs. Make sure they follow their outlines.

10. Model this process, and have students practice it many more times. You may decide to do "quick writes" of paragraphs as a type of daily language activity. Some subjects you may want to assign are:

> How to make the perfect sandwich
> My favorite weather conditions
> My favorite sport or hobby
> My best friend

How to make my favorite food

How to write a paragraph

My most embarrassing moment

The coolest animal

An awesome meal

What makes a good book

## Extensions and Modifications

Creating an outline template in which students fill in the blanks can be helpful:

I. Topic Sentence: _____

    A. Support sentence #1:_____

    B. Support sentence #2:_____

    C. Support sentence #3:_____

Have students place a finger or two between the margin and where they begin their topic sentences; this will help them to indent properly. Students who pick this up right away will probably be ready to dive into the essay format.

# Expository Writing Process: An Excellent Essay

**Purpose:** To introduce a model for developing nonfiction essays.

**Process:** Over a few days, as the teacher demonstrates the process, students compose essays.

**Payoff:** Students begin to meaningfully organize their writing.

**Phases:** Introduction, Guided Practice

## Standards Addressed

### English Language Arts

4. Students adjust their use of spoken, written, and visual language (e.g., conventions, style, vocabulary) to communicate effectively with a variety of audiences for a variety of purposes.

5. Students apply knowledge of language structure, language conventions (e.g., spelling and punctuation), media techniques, figurative language, and genre to create, critique, and discuss print and nonprint texts.

12. Students use spoken, written, and visual language to accomplish their own purposes (e.g., for learning, enjoyment, persuasion, and the exchange of information).

## Materials Needed

**Students Need:** "An Excellent Essay" handout (see page 9), notebook paper, pencils
**Teacher Needs:** Chart paper, markers

## Steps

1. Day One: Begin by explaining that a well-organized piece of writing is essential when expressing ideas to share with an audience. Explain that, over the next several days, every student will compose a nonfiction essay, following a specific format.

2. Distribute the handout.

3. Ask students to help you brainstorm several subjects on which you could write (for example, a recent trip, a pet, a momentous event). Write down the ideas on chart paper, leaving plenty of space between each idea.

4. With student help, under each subject generate three or four subtopics, that relate to the respective subject.

5. Instruct students to write down as many subjects as they can, with three or four subtopics each.

6. Day Two: With the class, choose a subject on which you will write. Copy the subject and respective topics on a new piece of chart paper, again leaving room between topics (you may want to post each of these pieces of chart paper in a conspicuous place).

> [subject:] My Trip to California
>     [topic I:] The Beach
>     [topic II:] The Amusement Park
>     [topic III:] Santa Cruz

7. Generate a list of supports for each subtopic.

> [subject:] My Trip to California
>     [topic I:] The Beach
>         [support A:] surfing
>         [support B:] sand crabs
>         [support C:] cotton candy
>     [topic II:] The Amusement Park etc.
>     [topic III:] Santa Cruz etc.

8. Have students help you compose a sentence for each subtopic, which will become the topic sentence for each "body" paragraph.

[subject:] My Trip to California
    [topic I:] The Beach: I really enjoyed the beach.
        [support A:] surfing
        [support B:] sand crabs
        [support C:] cotton candy
    [topic II:] The Amusement Park: Going to the Amusement Park was terrific, etc.
    [topic III:] Santa Cruz: I'll never forget my day in Santa Cruz, etc.

9. Assign students to pick a subject from their lists of brainstorms and write a sentence for each subtopic.

10. Day Three: Explain that each subtopic will be a paragraph in an essay about the subject and that the sentences written next to each subtopic are the topic sentences of the paragraphs in the body of the essay.

11. With student help, and using the outline, write out each paragraph, beginning with the topic sentence. Explain that, with some editing, the body of the essay is complete.

12. Have students complete the bodies of their essays.

13. Day Four: Explain that the next step is to create a topic paragraph, which, at the beginning of the essay, introduces the reader to the subject of the essay.

14. The first step is to create a thesis statement, or the subject of the essay put into a sentence (or the topic sentence of the topic paragraph). Have students help create a thesis statement for your work in progress.

[subject:] My Trip to California: I took a trip to California in May.

15. The next step is somewhat involved. Explain that a topic paragraph consists of each topic sentence from the body paragraphs, rewritten. Then have students help you rewrite your topic sentences on the chart paper with the outline.

[subject:] My Trip to California
    [topic A:] The Beach: I really enjoyed the beach.// A day at the beach was a special part of my trip.
        [subtopic 1:] surfing
        [subtopic 2:] sand crabs
        [subtopic 3:] cotton candy
    [topic B:] The Amusement Park: Going to the Amusement Park was terrific.// I loved the amusement park we visited, etc.
    [topic C:] Santa Cruz: I'll never forget my day in Santa Cruz.// Santa Cruz was a beautiful place to see, etc.

16. After each topic sentence has been rewritten, write each one in reverse order (C, B, A) after the thesis statement. (This allows for a smooth transition into the first body paragraph.)

> I took a trip to California in May. Santa Cruz was a beautiful place to see. I loved the amusement park we visited. A day at the beach was a special part of my trip.

17. Have students rewrite their topic sentences and compose their topic paragraphs.

18. Day Five: Now it is time to compose the concluding paragraph. This is the paragraph that explains what the person read. With student help, write a new version of the thesis statement. This becomes the topic sentence of the concluding paragraph. Next, rewrite the topic sentences of the body paragraphs yet again, but this time in the order in which they were presented (combining topic sentences is okay at this point).

19. Finally, have the class help you compose a concluding statement: a sentence that brings the entire essay to a close.

> My travels in the sunny state were spectacular.

20. Have students complete their own concluding paragraphs, edit, rewrite, and so forth.

21. Give students a chance to practice using this format many times during the school year. A terrific follow-up assignment, moving students into the Exercise phase, is to ask the students to write a complete essay about their families. Always encourage students to write about things that are familiar to them. Each family member gets a different body paragraph. Other possible essay subjects are:

How to spend the perfect day
My favorite sport
An autobiography (where students pick three main events in their lives)
My best friend
Rules for parents
How to make new friends
My pet
A funny thing happened to me

## Extensions and Modifications

Modified essay format (or "mini-essays") is more simply understood by some students. It entails a thesis statement, three body paragraphs, and a concluding statement. It might be a good place to start for some students. Once your students begin to "get" this, they may wish to play with the topic paragraph, to make it flow a little better. Instruction in effective transitions between paragraphs ("clinchers") may also be useful to advanced students.

Name:_____ Date: _____

# An Excellent Essay

I. Brainstorm a subject.

II. Write down at least three subtopics about the subject to discuss.
   —Write down information about each subtopic.
   —Write a topic sentence for each subtopic.
   —Write the rest of the paragraph for each idea, using the information you wrote down.
You now have the body of your essay complete!

III. Write a topic paragraph.
   —Rewrite each topic sentence (from II) in different words and add each one to the
      topic paragraph, in reverse order to the way the paragraphs will appear in your essay.
   —Write your thesis statement: a sentence that gives a summary of your whole essay.
      Put it at the beginning of the topic paragraph.
You have just completed your topic paragraph!

IV. Write a concluding paragraph, where you mention each idea in your topic paragraph.
   —Rewrite your thesis statement and make it the topic sentence of your concluding
      paragraph.
   —Rewrite your topic sentences a third time! You can combine topic sentences this
      time. Write them in the same order as your body paragraphs.
   —Add a final sentence that finishes off the essay In an interesting way. This is your
      concluding statement.

V. Edit, rewrite.

Thesis statement. Rewritten topic sentence number 3. Rewritten topic sentence number 2.
Rewritten topic sentence number 1.

Topic sentence #1. Rest of body paragraph number 1. _____
_____

Topic sentence #2. Rest of body paragraph number 2. _____
_____

Topic sentence #3. Rest of body paragraph number 3. _____
_____

Rewritten thesis statement. Re-rewritten topic sentence number 1. Re-rewritten topic
sentence number 2. Re-rewritten topic sentence number 3. Concluding statement.

*Lisa Kendall*
*Outline*

    I.  Dad—I love my dad.
        A. Divorced
        B. Job
        C. Name
        D. When with

    II.  Mom—My mom is pretty cool.
        A. Name
        B. Job
        C. When with
        D. Lives

    III.  Adam—I love my brother Adam.
        A. Age
        B. School
        C. Helps me
        D. Cheers up

    IV.  Kevin—I don't like Kevin at all.
        A. Age
        B. Nut case
        C. Acts
        D. Grade

### Family

I have a really cool family! Me and my brother Kevin are enemies. Me and Adam are best friends. I love my mom very much. I have a cool dad.

I love my dad. My dad divorced my mom. He works at AT&T. His real name is Brian. I'm with him all week, and every other weekend.

My mom is pretty cool! My mom's real name is Anne. She has two jobs, she is an insurance agent and a hairdresser! I'm with her every other weekend. She lives in the town homes.

I love my brother Adam! Adam is 13 years old. He goes to Chaparral. He helps me when I have a crisis on my hands. He cheers me up when I'm sad!

I don't like Kevin all of the time. Kevin is 8 years old. He's a real nutcase! He acts like prince charming around adults. He is in third grade.

I love my family! My mom and dad are really nice. Adam is very cool. I don't always get along with Kevin. If you don't like my family, tough nugget!

***Trevor Meyer***
***Outline***

    I. My dad and mom are very nice to me.
       A. Their emotions
       B. His moustache
       C. Dad's work

   II. My sister is very bratty.
       A. She's brattier but I love her
       B. She is in kindergarten
       C. She's vicious

  III. My grandparents spoil me rotten.
       A. My grandma really spoils me rotten
       B. My grandpa works in the garage
       C. My Nanna lives in Jacksonville

## *The Meyers*

My family is very kind. My grandparents are very nice to my sister and me. I love my sister even when she acts inappropriately. My mother and dad are very nice.

My mom and dad are very kind to me. They are mostly happy. My dad is growing a mustache. My dad works at Kaiser Permanente here in Colorado and in Kansas City.

My sister is very bratty but I love her very much. She is in kindergarten. When she doesn't get her way she gets vicious.

My grandparents spoil me rotten. My grandma is really the only one who spoils me. My grandpa loves to work in his garage. My Nanna lives in Jacksonville, Florida.

My family is the best. My parents have different levels of kindness. I love my sister because she's sort of cute, I love my Grandparents because they are nice to me. I'm proud to be a Meyer.

# Simple Short Story Format

**Purpose:**  To introduce the idea of an organized short story.

**Process:**  The teacher models the writing of an original story.

**Payoff:**  Students continue to meaningfully organize their writing.

**Phases:**  Introduction, Guided Practice

## Standards Addressed

### *English Language Arts*

4. Students adjust their use of spoken, written, and visual language (e.g., conventions, style, vocabulary) to communicate effectively with a variety of audiences for a variety of purposes.

5. Students apply knowledge of language structure, language conventions (e.g., spelling and punctuation), media techniques, figurative language, and genre to create, critique, and discuss print and nonprint texts.

12. Students use spoken, written, and visual language to accomplish their own purposes (e.g., for learning, enjoyment, persuasion, and the exchange of information).

## Materials Needed

**Students Need:**  Notebook paper, pencils

**Teacher Needs:**  Overhead projector, blank transparencies (or chart paper), several colors of overhead markers

## Steps

1. Day One: Explain to students that, although this is an intensely simplified way to write a short story, its format can eventually be altered to make a story more interesting.

2. With the class, brainstorm several possible story "problems" (pick something simple). One possible example is, "A cat is lost."

3. Brainstorm three, exactly three, events that will take place in your story, the third being the solution to the problem.

4. Explain that, in this simple story format, the first paragraph introduces the setting, characters, and problem; the three body paragraphs elaborate on three events; and the concluding paragraph summarizes the story. The introductory statement introduces the story in an interesting way.

5. Write an outline for the first four paragraphs:

    I. Introductory statement: Have you ever been lost?
       A. Setting: A large, cold, polluted city
       B. Characters: A polite and sad cat named Rio
       C. Problem: Rio is lost

II. Event 1: Rio needs to find food

    A. looks in trash cans

    B. tries to catch a mouse

    C. begs until a baker tosses her some bread

III. Event 2: Rio tries to find a place to stay warm

    A.

    B.

    C.

IV. Event 3 (solution): A little girl finds Rio

    etc.

6. Have the students brainstorm a fictional problem and three events that lead to a solution. Assist students in the development of their outlines.

7. Day Two: Quickly sketch how to write the story from the outline.

8. Write the concluding paragraph as if it were in essay format: Rewrite the introductory statement, summarize the three events, think up a snappy concluding statement.

9. Give students plenty of practice in writing a simple story. When they "get it," help them to modify the format by adding event paragraphs, introducing characters within the story (as events), putting an event paragraph before the introductory paragraph (to grab the reader), and so forth.

## Extensions and Modifications

Additional event paragraphs, focusing on creative vocabulary, and figurative language will make this task more challenging and interesting to higher-level writers.

# The Perfect Essay
# The Persuasive Essay

**Purpose:**  To assist students in creating persuasive works of nonfiction.

**Process:**  The teacher demonstrates the process as students compose essays.

**Payoff:**  Students meaningfully organize their writing for a specific purpose.

**Phases:**  Exercise, Application, Risk

## Standards Addressed

### *English Language Arts*

4. Students adjust their use of spoken, written, and visual language (e.g., conventions, style, vocabulary) to communicate effectively with a variety of audiences for a variety of purposes.

5. Students apply knowledge of language structure, language conventions (e.g., spelling and punctuation), media techniques, figurative language, and to create, critique, and discuss print and nonprint texts.

12. Students use spoken, written, and visual language to accomplish their own purposes (e.g., for learning, enjoyment, persuasion, and the exchange of information).

### *National Center for History in the Schools: Historical Thinking*

Standard 5. Historical Issues–Analysis and Decision-Making

D. Evaluate alternative courses of action.

E. Formulate a position or course of action on an issue.

### *Social Studies*

5. Individuals, Groups and Institutions: Social studies programs should include experiences that provide for the study of interactions among individuals, groups, and institutions.

## Materials Needed

**Students Need:**  "Persuasive Essay Planning Sheet" (see page 16), notebook paper, pencil

**Teacher Needs:**  Transparency of "Persuasive Essay Planning Sheet," overhead projector, blank transparencies, overhead markers

## Steps

1. Ask students what it means to persuade someone of something. Facilitate a discussion on which means of persuasion work and which do not. Ask students what they have read lately that attempted to persuade them of something and why it did or didn't work. You may wish to take notes of student responses on a transparency.

2. Explain to students that they are going to learn how to use the essay format to write a persuasive work. The format they use will be similar to essays they have been writing, but the way they plan will be different because the purpose of the essay is specific.

3. Hand out the planning sheet. Instruct students in the ways to create a good thesis statement, in this case, a "position." Tell them to write this statement in no uncertain terms. Xena IS stronger than Hercules. Summer IS better than winter. School lunch tastes AMAZING. In this first essay, give them a choice of these three topics on which to write:

>   TV is better than books.
>
>   Lunch time should be longer.
>
>   The school day should be shorter.
>
>   Tell them they must choose one of the above sentences as their thesis statements.

4. While you pick a position and model brainstorming convincing arguments for and against your thesis, have students do the same for theirs. The key is to think of as many as possible on both sides. Tell students that coming up with arguments against their own positions and figuring out ways to refute those arguments allows them to be more prepared to persuade.

5. Explain to students that you will pick two "pros" and a "con" to use in your body paragraphs, then circle the arguments you will use.

6. Create a body paragraph outline, with I. being your first "pro" argument. Jot down some supporting reasons for your first argument as A., B., and C. (please refer to the planning sheet). Do the same for II.

7. For your "con" argument, start the topic sentence for body paragraph number three (III.), with a phrase such as, "It's not true that ..." or "Some people say ..." or "You may think ..."; finish the sentence with the "con" argument. This allows you to address an argument against your position. Have the class come up with three ideas that shoot down the "con" argument. Write these down as A., B., and C.

8. Quickly review how to create a topic paragraph: Write the thesis statement, and rewrite the body paragraph topic sentences in reverse order.

9. Review the concluding paragraph: rewrite the thesis statement, rewrite the body paragraph topic sentences, and end with a powerful concluding statement.

## Extensions and Modifications

Once students get the hang of writing this first persuasive essay, you have many options. You may wish to give them other specific positions from which to choose or have them create their own thesis statements. I get a great deal of pleasure out of challenging my own students by assigning persuasive essays whose positions are exactly opposite to the ones they have just written. A good example of this is in the following pages.

Name:_____   Date: _____

# Persuasive Essay Planning Sheet

1. What is your thesis statement (Position)?

   _____

   _____

2. Write down arguments for (PRO) and against (CON) your statement:

   | PRO | CON |
   |---|---|
   |  |  |

3. Pick two "PROs" and three "CONs" to use.

4. Create the outline for your body paragraphs with your selections.

   I. PRO #1

   II. PRO #2

   III. CON #3 ("Some people say that ...," "It is not true that ...," etc.)

5. Write your body paragraphs, topic paragraph, and concluding paragraph.

**Ali Fraze**
**Final Draft**

T.V. is better than books. You may hear that reading is more relaxing than T.V., but that's not true. Special effects make T.V. and movies more interesting. Your useful time shouldn't be wasted reading some stupid book! So much stuff can be accomplished while you're watching T.V.

While you're watching T.V., you could do lots of other stuff. There's not enough time in the world to waste it reading some book. Let's say, when you come home from school, you have to read 50 pages in this really boring book, and it's your night to cook what can you do? You get the movie! You can eat dinner, you can cook, dinner, you could even read while you're watching T.V., especially when there are commercials.

Watching T.V. takes less time than reading. Some people take too much time reading over every word 10 times until it makes sense, especially people like me! T.V. gets people hooked because it's so interesting. This may result in getting it over with faster. A 500 page book can be seen in a two-hour movie!

T.V. is so much more interesting than reading some boring book. All of the special effects in today's movies really make them come to life. You can experience your favorite movies with all of your favorite stars. T.V. is lots of fun, especially game shows and other stuff you can participate in.

You may hear that reading is relaxing but that's not true. If you have a learning disability or something, reading could be very stressful. If you have a deadline, there might be a lot of pressure on you to finish the book and you might not get it done. Some books can be so relaxing (or boring) that they just put you to sleep.

As you can see, T.V. is a lot better than books. If you start watching more T.V., and read fewer books, you'll notice you're accomplishing so much more, and you're becoming a more relaxed, more interesting person. Hopefully, you'll start watching more T.V.

**Ali Fraze**
**Final Draft**

Books are better than T.V. Some people might say T.V. makes you a more interesting person, but that's not true. Books are great to take anywhere. Your children will sound like Shakespeare when they get to be your age. Books are educational and imaginative.

Educational books can fill your children's minds with imagination and fun. Why else would you spend years and years of your life learning how to read if it wasn't educational. It's always good to have fun and interesting books that make your mind make up the characters. With T.V. all of the characters are laid right in front of you, so you can't make anything up.

Everyday the vocabulary in children's books is getting bigger and bigger. If kids keep reading these educational books, the youngest people are going to be using the biggest words. Even if young kids don't understand all of the big words yet, as they repeatedly see these words they'll learn to understand them, and use this skill on bigger words. These words can be a big advantage in future school years. Getting great grades can be caused by learning these words early in life.

Starting at an early age you can read books practically anywhere. Books are great to take on trips. T.V.s are so big and they have so many wires. One hundred books would take up less space and weigh less than the average T.V.

You may hear that T.V. makes you a more interesting person, but that's not true. I've heard that watching too much T.V. could give you brain damage. With all of the violence on kids shows, you might as well take them to Columbia. Commercials give you the wrong ideas about many things, and you end up wasting a ton of money.

As you can see, books are a lot better than T.V. If you start reading more books, and watching less T.V., you'll find you're getting smarter, using bigger words, and even if you've heard that T.V. makes you a more interesting person, don't make up your mind until you've cut down on your T.V. watching.

## Do They Need It? An in depth look at recess
### Forward

After two hours and 15 minutes of hand cramps and writer's block (and a lot of soda) I went from information about each topic to a final draft (thank God for "Nick at Night"). I hope you enjoy this article and read my other article "A Brochure to Year-Round School."

Recess should be shorter. People say the students need exercise, and they do. If students get more time to learn, they'll need more time to work. If recess is shorter students will greatly benefit.

If recess is shorter, students will get more time to learn. Thirty-four minutes each day is spent on recess. That valuable time could be used on work or learning a lesson.

If students get more time to learn, then they'll need more time to work. Since next year, the 6th graders will not have a recess and will have a lot more work, being used to not having a recess would help them with their work now, and help them get ready for next year.

Some people say students need recess time to get our energy and exercise. P.E. (Physical Education) is taught to students in school already, so there is no reason to ruin perfectly good school time.

We don't need extra school time, we need less recess. People say kids need to have recess for exercise. The more students learn, the more time students need to work. If recess is shortened, there will be more time to teach. Don't let our kids lose out on a good education, recess should be shorter!

Name:_____ Date: _____

# Persuasive Essay Assessment

**Task**

You have been asked by the mayor of a town to persuade the townspeople that cars are better for transportation than horses. Write a five-paragraph essay, defending your position.

**Requirements**

    Provide a pros/cons list

    Provide an outline

    Write the essay

**Grading**

    You will be graded on these factors:

        Style (How convincing is your argument?)

        Organization (Did you use proper essay structure?)

        Language and Editing (Did you check your work?)

        Spelling (Use a dictionary)

    After you've written out your work, please check for:

    Spelling

    Punctuation

    Does it make sense?

| Pros: | Cons: |
|---|---|
|  |  |
|  |  |
|  |  |
|  |  |
|  |  |
|  |  |
|  |  |

# Editing Practice

**Purpose:** To give students many opportunities for editing written work.

**Process:** Students edit paragraphs on worksheets.

**Payoff:** Students recognize different types of errors that occur in writing.

**Phase:** Exercise

## Standards Addressed

### English Language Arts

5. Students apply knowledge of language structure, language conventions (e.g., spelling and punctuation), media techniques, figurative language, and genre to create, critique, and discuss print and nonprint texts.

## Materials Needed

**Students Need:** "Editing Practice" sheets (see pages 21–30), pencils

**Teacher Needs:** Transparencies of the "Editing Practice" sheets (see pages 21–30), overhead markers

## Steps

1. Hand out worksheets, have students individually edit the paragraphs.
2. When students have had time to complete each practice, go over that sheet on the overhead, having students come up and make the corrections.

## Extensions and Modifications

You may need to read what is written to students who are having difficulty or have them explain to you how to correct the errors. They may also wish to retype the paragraphs correctly on a computer.

Name:_____ Date: _____

## Editing Practice #1

Please find the errors in the following paragraph. Put a line through the error and write the correction above it. The number of errors in each line is given to you in the margin.

4    this weekend was perty awesome. Frist I got to sleep late, then I wached

3    superman on television. Their wasnt much food in the house for breakfast,

3    so I drink some coffee and ate tomato soup it was tasty and felt gud in my

4    belly. Next, I went back to sleep. Because I was tired. I slepped intil too

3    o'clock. Later, I go to a movie called lost in space. I was funny. I mad

4    yummy crab legs for dinner, and watch "Xena before I go to bed

Name:_____ Date: _____

## Editing Practice #2

Please find the errors in the following paragraph. Put a line through the error and write the correction above it. The number of errors in each line is given to you in the margin.

2    The weather condishuns from El Niño have caused problems all ovar the

4    world. In florida, many homes wear destroy Because of tornados. Some

4    place in California gets lost of rain last week. My mom lives in california.

2    She don't like all the damage the rain is causing in her city I feel sorry for

3    her. In denver, Colorado, were expecting big snowstorms but weave only

5    had one or too. in grand Juncshun, it has been warmr than past winters. El

3    Niño has stirred up trouble acros the globe. Don't forget to we're the rite

1    clothing each day

Name: **KEY**                                      Date: _____

## Editing Practice #1

Please find the errors in the following paragraph. Put a line through the error and write the correction above it. The number of errors in each line is given to you in the margin.

       This           pretty       First,                    watched

4    ~~this~~ weekend was ~~perty~~ awesome. ~~Frist~~ I got to sleep late, then I ~~wached~~

     "Superman"            There wasn't

3    ~~superman~~ on television. ~~Their wasnt~~ much food in the house for breakfast,

        drank                       . It        good

3    so I ~~drink~~ some coffee and ate tomato soup ~~it~~ was tasty and felt ~~gud~~ in my

               , because            slept until two

4    belly. Next, I went back to sleep. ~~Because~~ I was tired. I ~~slepped intil too~~

          went         "Lost in Space." It      made

3    o'clock. Later, I ~~go~~ to a movie called ~~lost in space. I~~ was funny. I ~~mad~~

                    watched "Xena"    went

4    yummy crab legs for dinner, and ~~watch "Xena~~ before I ~~go~~ to bed .

---

Name: **KEY**                                      Date: _____

## Editing Practice #2

Please find the errors in the following paragraph. Put a line through the error and write the correction above it. The number of errors in each line is given to you in the margin.

              conditions                            over

2    The weather ~~condishuns~~ from El Niño have caused problems all ~~ovar~~ the

        Florida        were destroyed because

4    world. In ~~florida~~, many homes ~~wear destroy Because~~ of tornados. Some

   places        got lots                 California

4    ~~place~~ in California ~~gets lost~~ of rain last week. My mom lives in ~~california.~~

      doesn't

2    She ~~don't~~ like all the damage the rain is causing in her city I feel sorry for

     Denver      we're               we've

3    her. In ~~denver~~, Colorado, ~~were~~ expecting big snowstorms but ~~weave~~ only

      two. In Grand Junction      warmer

5    had one or ~~too. in grand Juncshun~~, it has been ~~warmr~~ than past winters. El

            across                 wear   right

3    Niño has stirred up trouble ~~acros~~ the globe. Don't forget to ~~we're~~ the ~~rite~~

1    clothing each day .

Name:_____ Date: _____

# Editing Practice #3

Please find the errors in the following paragraph. Put a line through the error and write the correction above it. The number of errors in each line is given to you in the margin.

3    Have you every enjoyed a book soo much that you cant stop thinking

3    about it. Maybe it's story is magicle and stays with you. The writing in

3    book just amazes me sometime. Occasionally a book starts out kind of

5    slow, then get's better and better, until I cant but it down I've read books

2    that had awesome storys, but the writing was so awful that it takes away

2    from the fun. It doesnt really matter what makes a book spesial to you, as

1    long as you injoy it.

Name: **KEY**                                    Date: _____

# Editing Practice #3

Please find the errors in the following paragraph. Put a line through the error and write the correction above it. The number of errors in each line is given to you in the margin.

                  *ever*                *so*              *can't*

3     Have you ~~every~~ enjoyed a book ~~soo~~ much that you ~~cant~~ stop thinking

                    **?**       *its*        *magical*

3     about it, Maybe ~~it's~~ story is ~~magicle~~ and stays with you. The writing in

     *books*              *sometimes*

3     ~~book~~ just amazes me ~~sometime~~. Occasionally, a book starts out kind of

     *slowly*    *gets*                       *can't put*

5     ~~slow~~, then ~~get's~~ better and better, until I ~~cant but~~ it down. I've read books

                          *stories*                      *took*

2     that had awesome ~~storys~~, but the writing was so awful that it ~~takes~~ away

                    *doesn't*                        *special*

2     from the fun. It ~~doesnt~~ really matter what makes a book ~~spesial~~ to you, as

                  *enjoy*

1     long as you ~~injoy~~ it.

Name:_____ Date: _____

## Editing Practice #4

Please read the passage below and look at the underlined parts. Choose the answer with the best editing for each part.

Because <u>i was</u> in a hurry to leave for <u>nebraska</u> I didn't have a chance to make sure I packed everything I needed. I knew I had my <u>toothbrush razor, and comb.</u> Of course I remembered to pack underwear and <u>soxs I</u> can't believe that I <u>fergot</u> something so important! Have you ever gone on a trip and not brought the <u>write</u> shoes? Can you imagine <u>wearing</u> slippers with your very best clothes? I was very <u>embarrassed. Because</u> my shoes were so different from the rest of my outfit.

1. i were
   I were
   I was
   Correct as it is

2. Nebraska, I
   nebraska, I
   Nebraska I
   Correct as it is

3. Toothbrush razor and comb
   toothbrush, razor, and comb
   toothbrush, razor. And comb
   Correct as it is

4. soks, I
   socks. I
   sox. I
   Correct as it is

5. forget
   ferget
   forgot
   Correct as it is

6. rite
   right
   righte
   Correct as it is

7. wering
   wereing
   weareing
   Correct as it is

8. embarrssed cause
   embarrassed, because
   ambarrased. Because
   Correct as it is

Name: **KEY** _____    Date: _____

# Editing Practice #4

Please read the passage below and look at the underlined parts. Choose the answer with the best editing for each part.

Because <u>i was</u> in a hurry to leave for <u>nebraska</u> I didn't have a chance to make sure I packed everything I needed. I knew I had my <u>toothbrush razor, and comb.</u> Of course I remembered to pack underwear and <u>soxs I</u> can't believe that I <u>fergot</u> something so important! Have you ever gone on a trip and not brought the <u>write</u> shoes? Can you imagine <u>wearing</u> slippers with your very best clothes? I was very <u>embarrassed. Because</u> my shoes were so different from the rest of my outfit.

1. i were
   I were
   <u>I was</u>
   Correct as it is

2. <u>Nebraska, I</u>
   nebraska, I
   Nebraska I
   Correct as it is

3. Toothbrush razor and comb
   <u>toothbrush, razor, and comb</u>
   toothbrush, razor. And comb
   Correct as it is

4. soks, I
   <u>socks. I</u>
   sox. I
   Correct as it is

5. forget
   ferget
   <u>forgot</u>
   Correct as it is

6. rite
   <u>right</u>
   righte
   Correct as it is

7. wering
   wereing
   weareing
   <u>Correct as it is</u>

8. embarrssed cause
   <u>embarrassed, because</u>
   ambarrased. Because
   Correct as it is

Name:_____ Date: _____

# Editing Practice #5

Please read the passage below and look at the underlined parts. Choose the answer with the best editing for each part.

february 23, 1999

Dear Kathy,

  Can you believe how awesome are students our? I think it's very cool that these fourth graders are becoming more responsible Evry day. Are you getting sad to now? that we're so close to the end of the school year I am going to miss these students.

Your Very Good Friend,

  Eric

1.  February, 23 1999
    February, 23, 1999
    February 23, 1999
    Correct as it is

2.  Dear kathy,
    Dear, Kathy
    Dear Kathy
    Correct as it is

3.  our students are
    are students are
    our students our
    Correct as it is

4.  evry
    Evrey
    every
    Correct as it is

5.  now. That
    now that
    know that
    Correct as it is

6.  year? I
    year, I
    year I
    Correct as it is

7.  Your very good friend
    Your very good friend,
    You're Very Good Friend,
    Correct as it is

Name: **KEY**                                    Date: _____

# Editing Practice #5

Please read the passage below and look at the underlined parts. Choose the answer with the best editing for each part.

february 23, 1999

Dear Kathy,

 Can you believe how awesome are students our? I think it's very cool that these fourth graders are becoming more responsible Evry day. Are you getting sad to now? that we're so close to the end of the school year I am going to miss these students.

Your Very Good Friend,

 Eric

1. February, 23 1999
 February, 23, 1999
 February 23, 1999
 Correct as it is

2. Dear kathy,
 Dear, Kathy
 Dear Kathy
 Correct as it is

3. our students are
 are students are
 our students our
 Correct as it is

4. evry
 Evrey
 every
 Correct as it is

5. now. That
 now that
 know that
 Correct as it is

6. year? I
 year, I
 year I
 Correct as it is

7. Your very good friend
 Your very good friend,
 You're Very Good Friend,
 Correct as it is

Name:_____ Date: _____

## Editing Practice #6

Please read the passage below and look at the underlined parts. Choose the answer with the best editing for each part.

   My new cat's very <u>cute he's</u> black and tiny. We don't know if we should name him after a character from a <u>book cartoon, or</u> a movie. He likes to sleep under <u>my chin but wakes</u> me up at three in the morning by licking and biting my nose. In the <u>mornig he</u> attacks my feet. I love my new little <u>kitty tho</u> I wish <u>he would</u> sleep a little longer.

1. cute, his

   cute. He's

   cute. His

   Correct as it is

2. book, cartoon, or

   book or cartoon or

   book. Or Cartoon or

   Correct as it is

3. my chin but wake

   me chin, but wakes

   my chin, but wakes

   Correct as it is

4. the morning he

   morning, he

   mornig, he

   Correct as it is

5. kitty, though

   kitty though

   kitty, tho

   Correct as it is

6. he wood

   he. Would

   he would.

   Correct as it is

Name: KEY                                    Date: _____

## Editing Practice #6

Please read the passage below and look at the underlined parts. Choose the answer with the best editing for each part.

My new cat's very <u>cute he's</u> black and tiny. We don't know if we should name him after a character from a <u>book cartoon, or</u> a movie. He likes to sleep under <u>my chin but wakes</u> me up at three in the morning by licking and biting my nose. In the <u>mornig he</u> attacks my feet. I love my new little <u>kitty tho</u> I wish <u>he would</u> sleep a little longer.

1. cute, his

   <u>cute. He's</u>

   cute. His

   Correct as it is

2. <u>book, cartoon, or</u>

   book or cartoon or

   book. Or Cartoon or

   Correct as it is

3. my chin but wake

   me chin, but wakes

   <u>my chin, but wakes</u>

   Correct as it is

4. the morning he

   <u>morning, he</u>

   mornig, he

   Correct as it is

5. <u>kitty, though</u>

   kitty though

   kitty, tho

   Correct as it is

6. he wood

   he. Would

   he would.

   <u>Correct as it is</u>

# Novels

**Purpose:** To have students think about cause and effect relationships in literature.

**Process:** Over time, in their independent reading and in read–alouds, students discuss and write about cause and effect relationships.

**Payoff:** Students use cause and effect relationships to better understand what they are reading.

**Phases:** Application, Risk

## Standards Addressed

### *English Language Arts*

1. Students read a wide range of print and nonprint texts to build an understanding of texts, of themselves, and of the cultures of the United States and the world; to acquire new information; to respond to the needs and demands of society and the workplace; and for personal fulfillment. Among these texts are fiction and nonfiction, classic and contemporary works.

3. Students apply a wide range of strategies to comprehend, interpret, evaluate, and appreciate texts.

5. Students apply knowledge of language structure, language conventions (e.g., spelling and punctuation), media techniques, figurative language, and genre to create, critique, and discuss print and nonprint texts.

### *National Center for History in the Schools: Historical Thinking*

Standard 3. Historical Analysis and Interpretation

E. Analyze cause-and-effect relationships and multiple causation, including the importance of the individual, the influence of ideas, and the role of chance.

## Materials Needed

**Students Need:** Novels, "Reading Record" (see page 33), and "Novel Closure" sheets (see page 34–35), pencils

## Steps

1. Give students time, after independent reading, to write down cause and effect relationships in their reading records. Emphasize the importance of recognizing physical and emotional relationships. Physical cause and effect relationships are generally predictable.  (If you drop a glass on the floor, it will probably break.) Emotional cause and effect relationships are less predictable because they depend on human reactions.

2. During read–aloud time, ask questions about cause and effect relationships.

3. Provide opportunities for students to share causes and effects from their reading.

4. Use "Novel Closure" sheets to assess student comprehension.

## Extensions and Modifications

Obviously, appropriate choice of reading material will help students be successful in this pursuit.

Name: _____ Date: _____

## Reading Record

**Author:** _____

**Title:** _____

**Difficulty** (Easy, Just Right, Challenging): _____ **Type of Book:** _____

**Rating** (1 = worst – 5 =best): _____ **Number of Pages:** _____

**Date Started:** _____ **Date Finished/Abandoned:** _____

**Date:** _____ **Pages Read:** _____

_____

_____

_____

_____

**Date:** _____ **Pages Read:** _____

_____

_____

_____

_____

**Date:** _____ **Pages Read:** _____

_____

_____

_____

_____

**Date:** _____ **Pages Read:** _____

_____

_____

_____

_____

Name:_____ Date:_____

# Novel Closure

Book Title: _____

Author: _____

**Setting:**

_____

_____

_____

_____

_____

_____

_____

_____

_____

**Most important cause and effect relationships:**

_____

_____

_____

_____

_____

_____

**Main characters and descriptions:**

_____

_____

_____

_____

_____

_____

_____

_____

_____

_____

_____

_____

_____

_____

_____

_____

_____

_____

_____

_____

## Novel Closure continued

What did you think of the book (and why)?

_____

_____

_____

_____

_____

_____

_____

What other books would you recommend to someone who liked this book?

_____

_____

_____

_____

_____

_____

_____

Please draw a sketch of a scene from the book and explain it.

This illustration is about:

Describe something in your life that you remembered when reading this book.

_____

_____

_____

*Anna Marie Jordan*
*Hatchet Cause and Effect*

### Physical–

In Hatchet the young Brian is sent to live with his father in the summer and his mother in the winter. His father, whom he is now going to spend time with, lives over the Canadian border. His mother gives a tiny hatchet to go along. The pilot is in severe pain in the plane and soon has a heart attack and stinks up the cockpit of the Cessna 406 which is a bush plane. The heart attack of the pilot causes for the boy to have to drive the plane he tries the radio and he finally crashes into a L shaped lake.

### Emotional–

His mother demands a divorce which forces Brian the young boy of the two seething parents to fly back and forth. He had dreams and saw things he should have never seen. The divorce was enough for young Brian but the secret of his mom seeing someone. He could not stand it all. His mom is forced to drive him to the airport where he will fly to meet his father.

## Chapter 2
# Newspaper Lessons

## Introduction

"Can we have newspaper time?"

Newspapers are an extremely useful form of media. They are ever changing, always current, and cheap, and can be cut, drawn upon, abused, and recycled. Reading daily papers is also the easiest way for students to become informed citizens.

Newspapers are cheap (or free) and can be used daily or weekly. During the School Tools unit, you will need classroom sets of papers at least three times per week. Newspapers, as a consistent part of the weekly schedule, become terrific jump-off points for discussion, reading for information, critical thinking, persuasive writing, and entertainment.

The tool developed in this section is the ability to read and gather information from a paper. Students will learn how to navigate the complicated organization of a daily broadsheet or tabloid. They will explore the entire paper to get a feel for how it is put together. Learning the functions of different types of articles will allow students to understand the frame of mind in which to read. They will get practice following the stories of their choice over time and gleaning the main idea from the articles.

As a member of the advisory board of a local newspaper's "Newspaper in Education" department, I have become very aware of the great lengths to which a news organization will go to reach educators. Contact the "Newspaper in Education" department of your local newspaper for useful resources, curriculum guides, and classroom programs. Many papers also run forums and in-services to assist you in efficient use of the newspaper. Newspapers can and should be used across the curriculum.

# How to Clip and Save a Newspaper Article

**Purpose:** To instruct students in a method of collecting relevant articles while properly citing the source.

**Process:** Students will observe a demonstration.

**Payoff:** This introductory lesson will set expectations for all assignments in which parts of the newspaper are clipped and saved.

**Phase:** Introduction

## Standards Addressed

### *English Language Arts*

1. Students read a wide range of print and nonprint texts to build an understanding of texts, of themselves, and of the cultures of the United States and the world; to acquire new information; to respond to the needs and demands of society and the workplace; and for personal fulfillment. Among these texts are fiction and nonfiction, classic and contemporary works.

3. Students apply a wide range of strategies to comprehend, interpret, evaluate, and appreciate texts.

## Materials Needed

**Teacher Needs:**   A newspaper, scissors, glue, several sheets of notebook or typing paper

## Steps

1. Students gather around a central demonstration area, where materials have been collected.

2. Announce that several assignments using the newspapers will require the students to cut out articles and properly attach them to paper to save them for future reference.

3. No overview to newspaper formats should be given yet. Pick out an article of interest (preferably one that is continued on another page). Show students how to find the rest of the article.

4. Cut out the entire article, including the title.

5. Clip the date, the name of the newspaper, and the page numbers from the top of the page.

6. Using the minimum of glue possible (newsprint and glue can make a mess when used in excess), carefully glue the date, publication, and page numbers to the top of a page of paper.

7. Paste the rest of the article to the paper. This is the tricky part, because many articles are bigger than a sheet of paper. Show students how to trim articles, cut between paragraphs, and plan their positioning before gluing. Ask them to use one side of the sheet of paper only.

8. Use your model of exquisite clipping and gluing as the paragon of expectations by putting it on a wall for reference.

## Extensions and Modifications

A written checklist for students to follow may be helpful:

1. Cut out entire article.
2. Cut out date.
3. Cut out newspaper name.
4. Cut out page numbers.
5. Plan how you will glue your article by placing it on the paper before gluing (make sure it doesn't stick over the sides of the paper).
6. Cut between paragraphs if necessary.
7. Put a spot of glue on each corner of each piece.

# Newspaper Seek Sheets

**Purpose:**  To introduce students to the organization of newspapers.

**Process:**  Students will work in pairs to complete a search for different components of a newspaper.

**Payoff:**  Students will have become familiar with the arrangement of the paper.

**Phase:**  Introduction

## Standards Addressed

### English Language Arts

1. Students read a wide range of print and nonprint texts to build an understanding of texts, of themselves, and of the cultures of the United States and the world; to acquire new information; to respond to the needs and demands of society and the workplace; and for personal fulfillment. Among these texts are fiction and nonfiction, classic and contemporary works.

3. Students apply a wide range of strategies to comprehend, interpret, evaluate, and appreciate texts.

5. Students apply knowledge of language structure, language conventions (e.g., spelling and punctuation), media techniques, figurative language, and genre to create, critique, and discuss print and nonprint texts.

## *Social Studies*

10. Civic Ideals and Practices: Social studies programs should include experiences that provide for the study of the ideals, principles, and practices of citizenship in a democratic republic.

## Materials Needed

**Students Need:** A newspaper for every two students, a "Newspaper Seek Sheet" for every two students (see page 41), glue, scissors, sheets of paper, pencils

## Steps

1. Begin by having students explore their newspapers. Demonstrate how to read a broadsheet newspaper versus a tabloid. A broadsheet can be hard for students to handle at first. Teach them to read the paper a section at a time, folding the sheets back along the spine, then in half "hamburger style." Jill Scott, head of NIE at the *Denver Post*, says that students should learn to make the paper "snap" on that first fold across the spine. She has also said that when reading an interesting or upsetting piece of news kids should exclaim, "Can you believe this?" while slapping the paper with the backs of their fingers. Trust me, kids can really get into this. I had the bad luck last year to be discussing the merits of a broadsheet, not realizing that the side of the newspaper that was facing the class had a full-page ladies' underwear ad from the local department store. Several of my students actually said "That really is a 'broad' sheet." Oops. Ask students to keep their newspapers in order for the moment.
2. Distribute "Seek Sheets." Go through instructions with students. Remind them of proper clipping and gluing procedures.
3. Students work while you circulate, trying not to answer too many questions, thus allowing students to struggle a little and find their own solutions.

## Extensions and Modifications

Students may wish to create their own "Seek Sheets" after completing the original, challenging each other to find certain items in the newspaper. Some students may need direct prompts about where to find the items they are seeking.

Name:_____ Date: _____

# Newspaper Seek Sheet

**Instructions:** It's up to you to find every item on this list in the newspaper. First locate it, then cut it out and glue it on a piece of paper. (Remember to cut neatly and glue carefully!) Make sure you label each item, then check it off this list. Don't forget to read what you cut out!

- ❏ A comic strip that's funny
- ❏ A local news story
- ❏ Yesterday's high temperature in Cairo, Egypt
- ❏ A news item about another country
- ❏ A sport's score
- ❏ A photograph where you've drawn a moustache on someone
- ❏ An ad for a movie you'd like to see
- ❏ An article about some form of entertainment
- ❏ A puzzle
- ❏ A headline
- ❏ A letter to the editor
- ❏ Someone's opinion
- ❏ An ad for a job you'd like to have
- ❏ This newspaper's volume number, price, and publisher information

# Article Types

**Purpose:** To give students practice in identifying newspaper article purposes.

**Process:** Students are given definitions of three types of articles, find examples of each, then compare them in class discussion.

**Payoff:** Students will be able to recognize the difference between a news story, a feature, and an article.

**Phases:** Guided Practice, Exercise

## Standards Addressed

### English Language Arts

1. Students read a wide range of print and nonprint texts to build an understanding of texts, of themselves, and of the cultures of the United States and the world; to acquire new information; to respond to the needs and demands of society and the workplace; and for personal fulfillment. Among these texts are fiction and nonfiction, classic and contemporary works.

3. Students apply a wide range of strategies to comprehend, interpret, evaluate, and appreciate texts.

5. Students apply knowledge of language structure, language conventions (e.g., spelling and punctuation), media techniques, figurative language, and genre to create, critique, and discuss print and nonprint texts.

### National Center for History in the Schools: Historical Thinking

Standard 3. Historical Analysis and Interpretation

A. Identify the author or source of the historical document or narrative.

B. Compare and contrast differing sets of ideas, values, personalities, behaviors, and institutions.

C. Differentiate between historical facts and historical interpretations.

### Social Studies

5. Individuals, Groups and Institutions: Social studies programs should include experiences that provide for the study of interactions among individuals, groups, and institutions.

10. Civic Ideals and Practices: Social studies programs should include experiences that provide for the study of the ideals, principles, and practices of citizenship in a democratic republic.

## Materials Needed

**Students Need**:   A newspaper
**Teacher Needs**:   A newspaper

## Steps

1. Explain that articles in the newspaper can be classified into three categories: news story, feature, and editorial.
2. Discuss the definition of each, then have students locate examples in their newspapers.

   *News Story*: A news story should be written in an objective way. It provides factual information about events without expressing the writer's opinion.

   *Feature*: Feature stories tend to be about people's personal lives, fashion, culture, or entertainment. These articles can be lighthearted or serious. They have plenty of facts, but the opinion of the author may be evident.

   *Editorial*: An editorial expresses the opinions of the writer. It is usually placed in certain sections of the paper, to set it apart from factual stories. Some editorials express the opinions of the publishers, while others can be written by columnists or readers.

3. Once you are confident that most students have a general idea, make a three-column chart on the board (or better yet on a large piece of paper for further reference), with a different type of article heading each column. With the class, generate a comparison/contrast chart showing the characteristics of each.
4. For homework, have students write an article using one of the forms, labeling which type they used.

## Extensions and Modifications

An alternative assignment is to have students find another article in the paper, take it home, and write why it is a news story, feature, or editorial. Some students may wish to write about all three types of articles!

# Who, What, Where, When, Why, and How

**Purpose:** To introduce the format of a newspaper article.

**Process:** Students read articles and keep track of where they find the five "Ws" and the "H."

**Payoff:** As they become aware of where to find pertinent information, students will be able to figure out efficiently what is important in an article.

**Phases:** Introduction, Guided Practice

## Standards Addressed

### English Language Arts

1. Students read a wide range of print and nonprint texts to build an understanding of texts, of themselves, and of the cultures of the United States and the world; to acquire new information; to respond to the needs and demands of society and the workplace; and for personal fulfillment. Among these texts are fiction and nonfiction, classic and contemporary works.

3. Students apply a wide range of strategies to comprehend, interpret, evaluate, and appreciate texts.

5. Students apply knowledge of language structure, language conventions (e.g., spelling and punctuation), media techniques, figurative language, and genre to create, critique, and discuss print and nonprint texts.

### Social Studies

2. Time, Continuity and Change: Social studies programs should include experiences that provide for the study of the ways human beings view themselves in and over time.

3. People, Place and Environments: Social studies programs should include experiences that provide for the study of people, places, and environments.

5. Individuals, Groups and Institutions: Social studies programs should include experiences that provide for the study of interactions among individuals, groups, and institutions.

6. Power, Authority and Governance: Social studies programs should include experiences that provide for the study of how people create and change structures of power, authority, and governance.

7. Production, Distribution and Consumption: Social studies programs should include experiences that provide for the study of how people organize for the production, distribution, and consumption of goods and services.

8. Science, Technology and Society: Social studies programs should include experiences that provide for the study of relationships among science, technology, and society.

9. Global Connections: Social studies programs should include experiences that provide for the study of global connections and interdependence.

10. Civic Ideals and Practices: Social studies programs should include experiences that provide for the study of the ideals, principles, and practices of citizenship in a democratic republic.

## Materials Needed

**Students Need:** Newspapers, pencils, notebook paper, "Newspaper Activity Sheet" (see page 46)

## Steps

1. Ask students to select and silently read a newspaper article.

2. After most students have finished reading, encourage them to share with the class where in the article they found the most important information. Facilitate a discussion about what is important, distilling it down to who, what, where, when, why, and how.

3. Students write down the answers to the five "Ws" and "H" and in which part of the article they discovered that information.

4. When this work is complete, students share their discoveries. Eventually, draw an inverted triangle (that is, base at the top and vertex at the bottom) to graphically represent how newspaper articles are written with the most important information at the beginning. When editors cut for room, they start at the end, where the minute details are written.

5. For homework, send home the newspaper and the activity sheet for the student to try on their own.

## Extensions and Modifications

You may wish to give the students the choice of reading an article independently or in pairs, or to follow along as you read one aloud. Some students will need assistance in finding an appropriate article.

Name:_____ Date: _____

# Newspaper Activity Sheet

1. Choose an article to read.
   Title: _____

2. Answer the following questions, using complete sentences:

   Who is the article about? _____

   _____

   What is the article about? _____

   _____

   _____

   Where does the event in the article take place?_____

   _____

   When does the event in the article take place? _____

   _____

   How did the event occur (what were the causes)?_____

   _____

   _____

3. Choose three words from your article for this vocabulary page.

   Word Number 1 _____ What does it mean?

   _____

   How was it used in the article?_____

   _____

   Word Number 2 _____ What does it mean?

   _____

   How was it used in the article?_____

   _____

   Word Number 3 _____ What does it mean?

   _____

   How was it used in the article?_____

   _____

# Cause and Effect in the Newspaper

**Purpose:** To reinforce the idea that the study of cause and effect is important in gleaning information about events.

**Process:** The teacher reads a short article, and students help to discover causes and effects within the article. Students then work in small groups to seek cause and effect relationships in the comics.

**Payoff:** Students continue to practice recognizing cause and effect.

**Phase:** Application

## Standards Addressed

### *English Language Arts*

1. Students read a wide range of print and nonprint texts to build an understanding of texts, of themselves, and of the cultures of the United States and the world; to acquire new information; to respond to the needs and demands of society and the workplace; and for personal fulfillment. Among these texts are fiction and nonfiction, classic and contemporary works.

3. Students apply a wide range of strategies to comprehend, interpret, evaluate, and appreciate texts.

5. Students apply knowledge of language structure, language conventions (e.g., spelling and punctuation), media techniques, figurative language, and genre to create, critique, and discuss print and nonprint texts.

### *National Center for History in the Schools: Historical Thinking*

Standard 1. Chronological Thinking

A. Distinguish between past, present, and future time.

B. Identify in historical narratives the temporal structure of a historical narrative or story.

C. Establish temporal order in constructing historical narratives of their own.

Standard 3. Historical Analysis and Interpretation

E. Analyze cause-and-effect relationships and multiple causation, including the importance of the individual, the influence of ideas, and the role of chance.

J. Hypothesize the influence of the past.

Standard 5. Historical Issues–Analysis and Decision–Making

B. Marshal evidence of antecedent circumstances and contemporary factors contributing to problems and alternative courses of action.

C. Identify relevant historical antecedents.

D. Evaluate alternative courses of action.

## Materials Needed

**Students Need:** Newspapers, pencils, paper

## Steps

1. The teacher reads a selected article to the class.
2. While the teacher writes down class ideas under "physical" and "emotional" on the board, students call out cause and effect relationships they recognized.
3. When a sufficient number has been reached, students are instructed to work in groups of four on an article of their choice. Two on the team will look for "physical" cause and effect relationships, while the other two will write down "emotional" relationships. Next, they will make sure they agree, as a group, on their findings, including whether the relationships were "physical" or "emotional."
4. For homework, students take home the comics page and create a "cause and effect" T–chart by cutting out frames and gluing them to the chart.

## Extensions and Modifications

Again, assignment or assistance in finding an article of appropriate length and difficulty may be necessary.

# Newspaper Project Assesment

**Purpose:** To assess student understanding of the uses of newspapers.

**Process:** Students follow a news event over time, writing their impressions of each article in a journal.

**Payoff:** Students demonstrate their abilities in using the newspaper, as well as their skills in recognizing the main idea and cause and effect relationships.

**Phases:** Application, Risk

## Standards Addressed

### *English Language Arts*

1. Students read a wide range of print and nonprint texts to build an understanding of texts, of themselves, and of the cultures of the United States and the world; to acquire new information; to respond to the needs and demands of society and the workplace; and for personal fulfillment. Among these texts are fiction and nonfiction, classic and contemporary works.
3. Students apply a wide range of strategies to comprehend, interpret, evaluate, and appreciate texts.

4. Students adjust their use of spoken, written, and visual language (e.g., conventions, style, vocabulary) to communicate effectively with a variety of audiences for a variety of purposes.

5. Students apply knowledge of language structure, language conventions (e.g., spelling and punctuation), media techniques, figurative language, and genre to create, critique, and discuss print and nonprint texts.

12. Students use spoken, written, and visual language to accomplish their own purposes (e.g., for learning, enjoyment, persuasion, and the exchange of information).

### *National Center for History in the Schools: Historical Thinking*

Standard 1. Chronological Thinking

    A. Distinguish between past, present, and future time.

Standard 2. Historical Comprehension

    A. Reconstruct the literal meaning of a historical passage.

    B. Identify the central question(s) the historical narrative addresses.

    G. Draw upon visual, literary, and musical sources.

Standard 3. Historical Analysis and Interpretation

    A. Identify the author or source of the historical document or narrative.

    B. Compare and contrast differing sets of ideas, values, personalities, behaviors, and institutions.

    C. Differentiate between historical facts and historical interpretations.

    D. Consider multiple perspectives.

    E. Analyze cause-and-effect relationships and multiple causation, including the importance of the individual, the influence of ideas, and the role of chance.

    H. Hold interpretations of history as tentative.

Standard 5. Historical Issues–Analysis and Decision–Making

    A. Identify issues and problems in the past.

    B. Marshal evidence of antecedent circumstances and contemporary factors contributing to problems and alternative courses of action.

    C. Identify relevant historical antecedents.

    D. Evaluate alternative courses of action.

### *Social Studies*

2. Time, Continuity and Change: Social studies programs should include experiences that provide for the study of the ways human beings view themselves in and over time.

3. People, Place and Environments: Social studies programs should include experiences that provide for the study of people, places, and environments.

5. Individuals, Groups and Institutions: Social studies programs should include experiences that provide for the study of interactions among individuals, groups, and institutions.

6. Power, Authority and Governance: Social studies programs should include experiences that provide for the study of how people create and change structures of power, authority, and governance.

7. Production, Distribution and Consumption: Social studies programs should include experiences that provide for the study of how people organize for the production, distribution, and consumption of goods and services.

8. Science, Technology and Society: Social studies programs should include experiences that provide for the study of relationships among science, technology, and society.

9. Global Connections: Social studies programs should include experiences that provide for the study of global connections and interdependence.

10. Civic Ideals and Practices: Social studies programs should include experiences that provide for the study of the ideals, principles, and practices of citizenship in a democratic republic.

## Materials Needed

**Students Need:** "Newspaper Project" sheets (see page 51), "Scoring Guide" (see page 52), notebook paper, scissors, glue

## Steps

1. Distribute "Newspaper Project" sheets and "Scoring Guides."
2. Read through sheets and explain.
3. Set aside time each day papers are delivered for collecting and journaling.

## Extensions and Modifications

For many students, local sports teams articles are easy to follow. You may wish to encourage some students to focus on the world arena. At times, students might have to scour the paper for stories related to their topics, when nothing specifically addresses them. This happened to several of my students, when our local paper stopped publishing articles about U.S. soldiers in Bosnia. Needless to say, students who had family members serving in the Balkans were pretty peeved. The discussion that ensued about the role of the media was quite interesting.

Name:_____    Date: _____

# Newspaper Project

**Introduction:** Now that you're beginning to understand the function of newspapers, it's time for you to begin a project that will give you practice in getting information, figuring out what's important, and communicating your understanding. Please read this entire page carefully.

These are the steps to take for an excellent project:

1. Select a news item you will follow. Make sure it's a story that will probably continue for several weeks.

2. Every day we have a paper, cut out the article(s) on your subject. Look for any related articles, editorials, or advertisements. Mount all items on notebook paper properly (with date and name of newspaper). Underline the main idea in each paragraph.

3. On another piece of notebook paper, keep a running journal of what happened. Write down your thoughts about the article and answer questions such as:

   What were the causes of the event?
   What led to the event?
   What were (or are) the effects (long term and short term)?
   How could the effects have been different?
   What is the main idea of this article?

4. Look for more information on your subject in magazines and on the TV news. Document your findings in your journal. Don't forget to date each entry and properly cite where you found your information.

5. After meticulously following your news item, cutting out all related articles, and keeping a journal, you'll write a chronology of the events. You will also include a short summary, explaining as many cause and effect relationships as possible. This, and your journal entries, will demonstrate how well you understand cause and effect, as well as what you read. Please see the "Scoring Guide for Newspaper Project" for more details.

# Scoring Guide for Newspaper Project

| | Exceptional | Proficient | In Progress |
|---|---|---|---|
| **Understanding of Main Idea** | Every journal entry clearly expresses the main idea of each article. | Every journal entry mentions the main idea of each article. | Some journal entries do not mention the main idea of the article. |
| **Understanding of Event's Cause and Effect** | Chronology and final summary list multiple physical and emotional effects of the event. | Chronology and final summary list some physical causes and effects of the event. | Chronology and final summary list few or no causes and effects of the event. |
| **Organization and Presentation** | Every entry consists of: entire article, which is neatly attached without extending beyond the page, date, publication name, underlining of main idea in each paragraph, and a neatly written journal entry.<br><br>Entire project is in proper order and is easy to read. | Every entry consists of: entire article, which is neatly attached, as well as 3 out of the following: date, publication name, underlining of main idea in each paragraph, a neatly written journal entry.<br><br>Entire project is in proper order and is easy to read. | Some entries do not consist of entire article, neatly attached, or are missing one of the following: date, publication name, underlining of main idea in each paragraph, a neatly written journal entry.<br><br>Project is not in proper order or easy to read. |

## Chapter 3

# Mathematics Lessons

## Introduction

### Three Essential Tools for Student Success

The following lessons focus on three basic tools students will be able to use right away. Map skills are multifaceted. Not only do they work to help students understand the basics of scale, but they also allow the student a deeper understanding of related cause and effect relationships in geography. The ability to quickly use basic multiplication has a huge effect on a student's facility with problem solving in mathematics, both in the classroom and at the local music store. Finally, learning to express one's understanding in mathematics problem solving is essential.

The lessons on map skills become progressively more involved. The parallel between scale drawing and scale maps allows students to connect the mathematical concepts involved in both. A classroom set of world atlases is very helpful during this unit. I also got my hands on a classroom set of state maps from the local auto club. After laminating these, my students were able to write on them with dry erase markers. They are a valuable tool across the curriculum. Understanding how maps are read and the information they communicate allows students to apply this knowledge to the social studies curriculum. So many of the cause and effect relationships in human history are based on proximity, physical geography, and cultural geography. A student who can gather information from maps becomes well informed about the influences of geography on the social sciences.

Math facts, especially the multiplication tables, are essential long-term knowledge. Rote memorization is not always a bad thing! Once students fully understand the concept of multiplication, the only thing left to do is practice. Although many useful mnemonics exist for learning fact families, in the end, only consistent, goal-oriented drills will help students readily employ the facts.

Communicating a problem-solving process is an upper-level skill, essential for mathematical reasoning. In the format provided, students have the opportunity to solve problems, then write formal "reports" about their travails.

# Full Text
# of Relevant NCTM Standards

4. Mathematical Power

   The assessment of students' mathematical knowledge should yield information about their—

   - ability to apply their knowledge to solve problems within mathematics and other disciplines;
   - ability to use mathematical language to communicate ideas;
   - ability to reason and analyze;
   - knowledge and understanding of concepts and procedures;
   - disposition toward mathematics;
   - understanding of the nature of mathematics;
   - integration of these aspects of mathematical knowledge.

5. Problem Solving

   The assessment of students' ability to use mathematics in solving problems should provide evidence that they can—

   - formulate problems;
   - apply a variety of strategies to solve problems;
   - solve problems;
   - verify and interpret results;
   - generalize solutions.

6. Communication

   The assessment of students' ability to communicate mathematics should provide evidence that they can—

   - express mathematical ideas by speaking, writing, demonstrating, and depicting them visually;
   - understand, interpret, and evaluate mathematical ideas that are presented in written, oral, or visual forms;
   - use mathematical vocabulary, notation, and structure to represent ideas, describe relationships, and model situations.

8. Mathematical Concepts

   The assessment of students' knowledge and understanding of mathematical concepts should provide evidence that they can—

   - label, verbalize, and define concepts;
   - identify and generate examples and nonexamples;
   - use models, diagrams, and symbols to represent concepts;
   - translate from one mode of representation to another;
   - recognize the various meanings and interpretations of concepts;

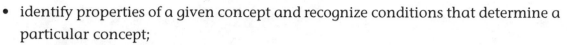

- identify properties of a given concept and recognize conditions that determine a particular concept;
- compare and contrast concepts.

9. Mathematical Procedures

The assessment of students' knowledge of procedures should provide evidence that they can—

- recognize when a procedure is appropriate;
- give reasons for the steps in a procedure;
- reliably and efficiently execute procedures;
- verify the results of procedures empirically (e.g., using models) or analytically;
- recognize correct and incorrect procedures;
- generate new procedures and extend or modify familiar ones;
- appreciate the nature and role of procedures in mathematics.

10. Mathematical Disposition

The assessment of students' mathematical disposition should seek information about their—

- confidence in using mathematics to solve problems, to communicate ideas, and to reason;
- flexibility in exploring mathematical ideas and trying alternative methods in solving problems;
- willingness to persevere in mathematical tasks;
- interest, curiosity, and inventiveness in doing mathematics;
- inclination to monitor and reflect on their own thinking and performance;
- valuing of the application of mathematics to situations arising in other disciplines and everyday experiences;
- appreciation of the role of mathematics in our culture and its value as a tool and as a language.

# Room Scale

**Purpose:** To give students practice using the concept of "scale."
**Process:** Students will make a simple scale drawing of the room.
**Payoff:** Students have the chance to practice working with scale in a kinesthetic way.
**Phases:** Introduction, Guided Practice

## Standards Addressed

### Geography

The geographically informed person knows and understands:

1. How to use maps and other geographic representations, tools, and technologies to acquire, process, and report information from a spatial perspective.
2. How to use mental maps to organize information about people, places, and environments in a spatial context.
3. How to analyze the spatial organization of people, places, and environments on earth's surface.
4. The physical and human characteristics of places.

### Mathematics

4. Mathematical Power
6. Communication
8. Mathematical Concepts
9. Mathematical Procedures
10. Mathematical Disposition

## Materials Needed

**Students Need:** Graph paper, pencils, measurement tools (both standard and nonstandard)

## Steps

1. Have students gather; facilitate discussion on the meaning of scale. Use questions such as:

   What does the word *scale* mean?
   What does it mean when you are using a map?
   How big would a map of the United States have to be if it were not drawn to scale?
   Would you be able to take that map on a road trip?
   What are some different ways that scale is used?
   Where can the scale be found on a map?
   What units are often used in a scale?

2. On graph paper, demonstrate how you would make a scale drawing of an object (table, desk), using your hand as the unit of measurement.

3. Instruct students to work in pairs to make a scale drawing of the room. Inform them that no two groups may use the same measurement tool. That is, each group must clear the measurement tool with you first! This will encourage problem solving with nonstandard tools and diverse thought. Students may use books, shoes, string, pencils, and so forth.

4. Although this is a pre-assessment, many students will need direction in how to assign graph paper boxes a certain unit of length.

5. After students have completed the exercise, gather them to debrief. Discuss problems and solutions, brainstorms, and so forth.

6. Collect drawings to see who "gets it."

## Extensions and Modifications

You may need to work closely with certain students, or make the assignment more manageable (say, sketch a model of the shape of the room, roughly to scale, or just measure the walls, paying no attention to nooks and various other anomalies that show up in classrooms). Some students will be ready to add scale sketches of furniture to their drawings.

# Scale Drawings

**Purpose:**  To practice using the concept of scale.

**Process:**  Students will design rough and final drafts of posters.

**Payoff:**  Students gain understanding through practice.

**Phases:**  Guided Practice, Exercise

## Standards Addressed

### Geography

The geographically informed person knows and understands:

1. How to use maps and other geographic representations, tools, and technologies to acquire, process, and report information from a spatial perspective.
2. How to use mental maps to organize information about people, places, and environments in a spatial context.

### Mathematics

5. Problem Solving
6. Communication
8. Mathematical Concepts
9. Mathematical Procedures

## Materials needed

**Students Need:**   Rulers, pencils, slips of paper

## Steps

1. Explain to students that they will be creating a poster of the novels they are reading. They will need to draw a rough draft on the small paper, then a scale drawing of their rough draft on the larger paper. Ask students to share how this could be done.
2. Make sure they are on the right track and set them to work. Circulate to see how students are doing.

## Extensions and Modifications

As needed, have students draw their rough drafts on graph paper, then lightly draw grid marks onto the larger sheet. Next, they should copy their posters block by block. Some students may need you to actually copy the book cover, then draw a grid over it for them to use. If kids are really "getting it," have them make their rough drafts more complicated.

# Map Scale

**Purpose:** To introduce or review the use of scale maps.

**Process:** Students will complete a worksheet, using an atlas.

**Payoff:** Students have the chance to use what they have learned to practice working with scale.

**Phases:** Introduction, Guided Practice, Exercise

## Standards Addressed

### Geography

The geographically informed person knows and understands:

1. How to use maps and other geographic representations, tools, and technologies to acquire, process, and report information from a spatial perspective.
2. How to use mental maps to organize information about people, places, and environments in a spatial context.
3. How to analyze the spatial organization of people, places, and environments on earth's surface.
4. The physical and human characteristics of places.

### Mathematics

4. Mathematical Power
6. Communication
8. Mathematical Concepts
9. Mathematical Procedures

## Materials needed

**Students Need:** "Scale Drill" worksheet with page number of world map filled in; (see page 60), pencils, slips of paper, atlases

## Steps

1. Review the concept of scale maps with the class.
2. Show students how to make a scale ruler with a map scale and a slip of paper.
3. Explain to students how to complete the worksheet.
4. Ask students to work individually on sheets.

## Extensions and Modifications

You may need to create the scale ruler for some students. Students who finish quickly might enjoy finding distances between interesting places and writing them on the back.

Name:_____ Date: _____

# Scale Drill

Using the various scales of the maps named below, answer the following questions:

1. Using a world map, what is the distance in miles from Washington D.C. to Reykjavik, Iceland? _____

2. What is the distance in miles from Cape Town, South Africa to Shanghai, China? _____

3. What is the distance in kilometers from Los Angeles, California to Madrid, Spain? _____

4. Is the scale of the map of Middle America the same as the world map? _____

5. Using the Middle America map, what is the distance in miles from Mexico City, Mexico to Tegucigalpa, Honduras? _____

6. What is the distance in miles from Mexico City, Mexico to Havana, Cuba? _____

7. Using the map of Africa, what is the distance in miles from Johannesburg, South Africa to Cairo, Egypt? _____

8. What is the same distance in kilometers? _____

Name: **KEY**                                         Date: _____

# Scale Drill

Using the various scales of the maps named below, answer the following questions:

1. Using a world map, what is the distance in miles from Washington D.C. to Reykjavik, Iceland? **4,700 miles**

2. What is the distance in miles from Cape Town, South Africa to Shanghai, China?
   **9,000 miles**

3. What is the distance in kilometers from Los Angeles, California to Madrid, Spain?
   **13,000 km**

4. Is the scale of the map of Middle America the same as the world map?
   **No**

5. Using the Middle America map, what is the distance in miles from Mexico City, Mexico to Tegucigalpa, Honduras? **880 miles**

6. What is the distance in miles from Mexico City, Mexico to Havana, Cuba?
   **1,700 miles**

7. Using the map of Africa, what is the distance in miles from Johannesburg, South Africa to Cairo, Egypt? **4,000 miles**

8. What is the same distance in kilometers? **6,700 km**

# Latitude and Longitude:
# Grid Maps

**Purpose:** To give students a chance to learn the concept of grid maps in an enjoyable way.

**Process:** Students create grid maps, then play "Alien Attack" with them.

**Payoff:** By practicing with these grids, students are on their way toward reading longitude and latitude on maps.

**Phases:** Introduction, Exercise

## Standards Addressed

### Geography

The geographically informed person knows and understands:

1. How to use maps and other geographic representations, tools, and technologies to acquire, process, and report information from a spatial perspective.

2. How to use mental maps to organize information about people, places, and environments in a spatial context.

3. How to analyze the spatial organization of people, places, and environments on earth's surface.

### Mathematics

4. Mathematical Power

6. Communication

8. Mathematical Concepts

9. Mathematical Procedures

10. Mathematical Disposition

## Materials needed

**Students Need:**  Graph paper, pencils

## Steps

1. Ask students to explain how they know where to find places on maps. Talk about the use of the index in an atlas and how it shows the latitude and longitude of locations. Explain to students that they will be creating their own maps, using coordinates, to make a grid.

2. Demonstrate making a grid map, using letters for the horizontal axis (point out that letters, in this case, should fall on the lines, as opposed to the spaces) and numbers for the vertical axis. Have students do the same.

3. When students have finished creating their grids, demonstrate how to play "Alien Attack": Students pair up and secretly place their "space ships" on the graph drawn

in pencil. Each of four ships takes up a certain number of coordinates, as follows: 2 = Saucer; 3= Invader; 4 = Cruiser; 5 = Colonist. Next, students, in turn, "take shots" at each other by calling out coordinates. The opposing student responds with "hit" or "miss." Students keep track of their own shots with "Os," and their opponents' shots with "Xs," until one student has destroyed all of the others' space ships. A ship has been destroyed when the opponent has called out all of the coordinates that it covers.

## Extensions and Modifications

Some students will need a great deal of assistance creating their game boards and placing their vessels, while others may play multiple games.

# Latitude and Longitude: World Maps

**Purpose:** To allow students to develop deeper schema around latitude and longitude.

**Process:** Students create their own grids, then sketch out the continents on them.

**Payoff:** By making their own world maps, students' understanding of latitude and longitude will increase.

**Phases:** Guided Practice, Exercise

## Standards Addressed

### Geography

The geographically informed person knows and understands:

1. How to use maps and other geographic representations, tools, and technologies to acquire, process, and report information from a spatial perspective.

2. How to use mental maps to organize information about people, places, and environments in a spatial context.

3. How to analyze the spatial organization of people, places, and environments on earth's surface.

### Mathematics

4. Mathematical Power

8. Mathematical Concepts

9. Mathematical Procedures

## Materials Needed

**Students Need:**   Graph paper, pencils, atlases

## Steps

1. Use examples of different map projections in an atlas to talk about changing a spherical object to two dimensions. You may wish to peel an orange and trace it out to demonstrate. I draw various shapes onto the orange, then draw panels (straight lines from pole to pole). I explain that I am drawing lines of longitude. Next, I cut the panels with a knife, carefully slicing the peel but not the fruit. When I have the entire orange peeled, I place the peel pieces side by side in their proper order on paper, then trace them. This gives students the general idea of the difficulties of transferring the properties of round objects to paper.

2. On a piece of graph paper, create a grid of lines of longitude and latitude.

3. Ask students to do the same, then carefully mark the farthest northern-, southern-, eastern-, and western-most points of all the continents.

4. Students then sketch in the outlines of the continents.

5. Students compare their work with others to check for accuracy.

## Extensions and Modifications

Some students may do better with a copied map, where the longitude and latitude lines are already labeled. Then, individual guidance may be necessary as they find and place the extremities of each continent. If students pick this up right away, have them label extremities of major countries, then sketch them out and color their maps.

# Novel Use of Scale

**Purpose:** To allow students to work with more scale maps.

**Process:** Students keep track of distances characters travel, using the map from a novel.

**Payoff:** Understanding of scale is assessed.

**Phases:** Exercise, Application

## Standards Addressed

### English Language Arts

3. Students apply a wide range of strategies to comprehend, interpret, evaluate, and appreciate texts

### Geography

The geographically informed person knows and understands:

1. How to use maps and other geographic representations, tools, and technologies to acquire, process, and report information from a spatial perspective.
2. How to use mental maps to organize information about people, places, and environments in a spatial context.

### Mathematics

4. Mathematical Power
5. Problem Solving
6. Communication
8. Mathematical Concepts
9. Mathematical Procedures
10. Mathematical Disposition

## Materials Needed

**Students Need:** A "Character Travel Log" (see page 67), rulers, pencils, string, and a fiction book with a map in it. Some suggestions are:

- The "Redwall" Series by Brian Jacques, published by Putnam & Grosset Group (1986)
- *The Book of Three, The Black Cauldron,* and other series books by Lloyd Alexander, published by Holt, Rinehart & Winston (1964)
- The series starting with *Gom on Windy Mountain* by Grace Chetwen, published by Lothrop, Lee & Shepard (1986)
- *The Hawks of Fellheath* by Paul R. Fisher, published by Atheneum (1980)
- *Dinotopia* by James Gurney, published by Turner Publishing (1992)
- *The Phantom Tollbooth* by Norton Juster, published by Random House (1961)

- *The Hobbit* and *The Lord of the Rings* series by J. R. R. Tolkien, published by Ballantine (1954)
- The "Earthsea" series by Ursula K. Le Guin, published by Bantam (1968)
- *The Wind in the Willows* by Kenneth Grahame, published by Scribner's (1908)
- *Naya Nuki* and other books about Native Americans by Kenneth Thomasma, published by Grandview Publishing (1983)

**Note:** This is just a small list of the many books with maps. If you give your students time in the library, they'll find them!

## Steps

1. Instruct the students to keep a log, as they read the book, of where the characters go. They may have to make guesses for distances or use the times it took for the characters to travel.

## Extensions and Modifications

If you have read the book the students are reading, you may wish to map out the journey of the main character to prompt students who are having trouble. Also, a separate copy or sketch of the map may be helpful for students as they read the novel.

Name:_____  Date: _____

# Character Travel Log

Book Title:_____

Author: _____

| Character: | From: | To: | Distance: |
|---|---|---|---|
|  |  |  |  |
|  |  |  |  |
|  |  |  |  |
|  |  |  |  |
|  |  |  |  |
|  |  |  |  |
|  |  |  |  |
|  |  |  |  |
|  |  |  |  |
|  |  |  |  |
|  |  |  |  |
|  |  |  |  |
|  |  |  |  |
|  |  |  |  |
|  |  |  |  |

# Playground Scale Assessment

**Purpose:** To assess group understanding of the concept of scale.

**Process:** In groups, students create a scale drawing of the school playground.

**Payoff:** Students demonstrate their skills in making scale maps.

**Phases:** Application, Risk

## Standards Addressed

### Geography

The geographically informed person knows and understands:

1. How to use maps and other geographic representations, tools, and technologies to acquire, process, and report information from a spatial perspective.
2. How to use mental maps to organize information about people, places, and environments in a spatial context.
3. How to analyze the spatial organization of people, places, and environments on earth's surface.
4. The physical and human characteristics of places.

### Mathematics

4. Mathematical Power
5. Problem Solving
6. Communication
8. Mathematical Concepts
9. Mathematical Procedures
10. Mathematical Disposition

## Materials Needed

**Students Need:** Graph paper, pencils, measurement tools

## Steps

1. Explain to students that you will be assessing their abilities to create scale maps (review, if necessary).
2. Ask students to work in pairs or trios to create scale maps of the playground. Remind them that their scales must be present on the map.

## Extensions and Modifications

Some students may prefer to draw scale models of certain areas of the playground, while others may wish to go into detail.

# Plan a Voyage Assessment

**Purpose:** To assess student understanding of the concept of "scale."

**Process:** Students will plan a trip, using maps.

**Payoff:** Students demonstrate ability to use scale maps.

**Phase:** Application

## Standards Addressed

### Geography

The geographically informed person knows and understands:

1. How to use maps and other geographic representations, tools, and technologies to acquire, process, and report information from a spatial perspective.
2. How to use mental maps to organize information about people, places, and environments in a spatial context.
3. How to analyze the spatial organization of people, places, and environments on earth's surface.
4. The physical and human characteristics of places.

### Mathematics

4. Mathematical Power
5. Problem Solving
6. Communication
8. Mathematical Concepts
9. Mathematical Procedures

## Materials Needed

**Students Need:** "Plan a Voyage!" sheets (see page 70), pencils, string or rulers, atlases

## Steps

1. Have students plan a voyage with at least 10 legs, writing down their itinerary on the sheets.
2. To grade these, take a strip of paper and create a scale ruler.

## Extensions and Modifications

Five legs may be more realistic for some students. Others may wish to write details about their trips on a separate piece of paper. They might write about the time it could take to get to each destination, why they'd like to go to those places, and so forth. This assessment can be expanded into a problem-solving report (see page 83) or into an individual study of countries and attractions that such a voyage would have to offer.

Name:_____    Date:_____

# Plan a Voyage!

**Instructions:** Please fill in all of the distances for this trip, from using a map. Next, figure the total miles traveled, and fill in the box.

Once you've finished, please make a plan of how much the trip will cost on the back of this page. You'll need to estimate some prices.

| Date: | From: | To: | Distance: |
|-------|-------|-----|-----------|
|       |       |     |           |
|       |       |     |           |
|       |       |     |           |
|       |       |     |           |
|       |       |     |           |
|       |       |     |           |
|       |       |     |           |
|       |       |     |           |
|       |       |     |           |
|       |       |     |           |
|       |       |     |           |
|       |       |     |           |
|       |       |     |           |
|       |       |     | **Total:** |

# Multiplication Facts Practice

**Purpose:**  To give students ways to practice their math facts, for faster use.

**Process:**  Students are drilled weekly, while being responsible for practicing with flash cards at home.

**Payoff:**  By being able to think quickly of multiplication facts, mathematical problem solving should not be bogged down with algorithm traffic.

**Phase:**  Exercise

## Standards Addressed

### *Mathematics*

 4. Mathematical Power
 8. Mathematical Concepts
 9. Mathematical Procedures
10. Mathematical Disposition

## Materials Needed

**Students Need:**  Sets of "Multiplication Flash Cards" (see pages 73–75) on tagboard (You may wish to copy the included templates, or rewrite them on full, marginless 8 x 11 inch sheets.), "Math Facts Drill Sheets" (see pages 76–78), "Math Facts Flash Card Calendars" (see page 79), "Math Facts Tracking Sheet" (see page 80), scissors, colored pen for each student

**Teacher Needs:**  Overhead set of multiplication flash cards, red overhead pen

## Steps

1. Using red overhead pen, fill in blank corner of flash cards with products on overhead projector. Make sure students are doing so carefully, with you. For example, if one corner already says 2, and the other has a 3, then in the blank corner, you'll mark a 6.

2. Teach students to use the cards. By holding each card by a vertex and covering up the red answer, you leave the two factors, which when multiplied become the answer. Conversely, by holding the card by another vertex, you create a division problem with the dividend and divisor.

3. Pass out weekly calendars. Explain to students that their parents must initial each day they practice for the designated time and sign the bottom.

4. Distribute "Math Facts Tracking Sheet." Have students fill in the blanks, setting a goal every time they take timed drills.

5. Give a math facts drill once or twice per week and have students keep track of their results. Multiplication math drills are included in this book.

## Extensions and Modifications

I have made a deal with my students that, when they complete a drill in a given time four weeks in a row, they have "graduated" and only have to complete that drill once per month (to make sure they are staying current). Some of my students have graduated from all three operations and play math games while the rest of the class takes its drills. Folding the drill sheet in half during testing or giving students unlimited time to finish can make the task less daunting.

Name:_____ Date: _____

**Multiplication Flash Cards**          Score: _____ Time: _____

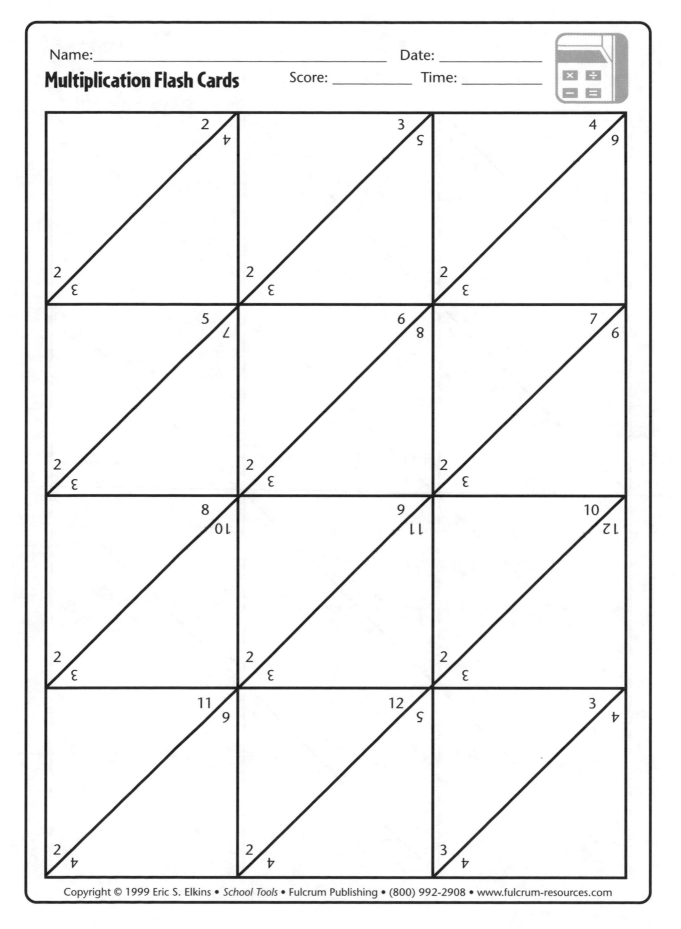

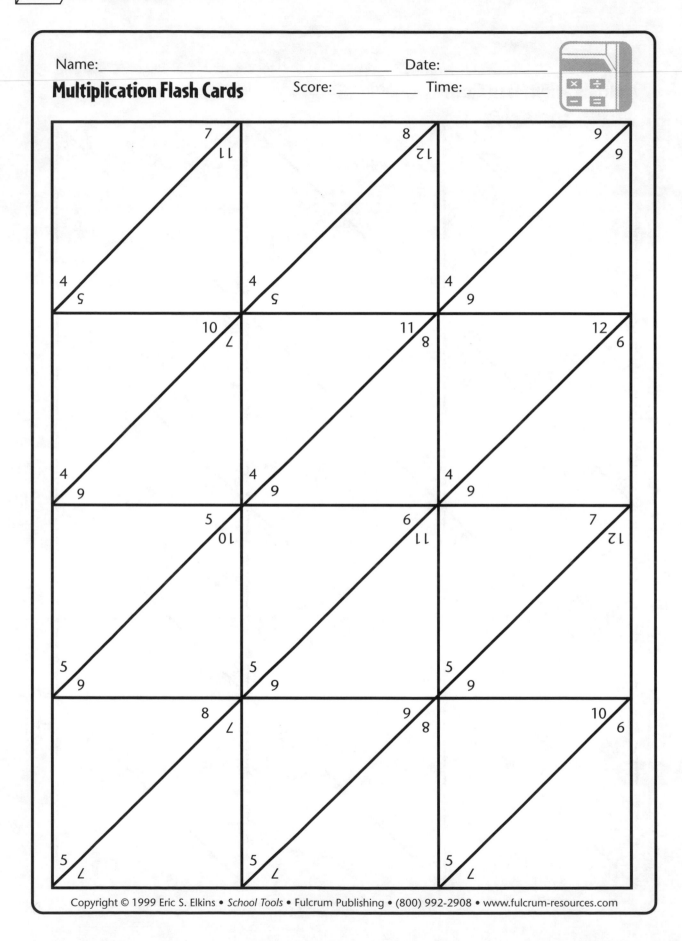

**Name:**_____    **Date:**_____

# Multiplication Flash Cards

**Score:**_____    **Time:**_____

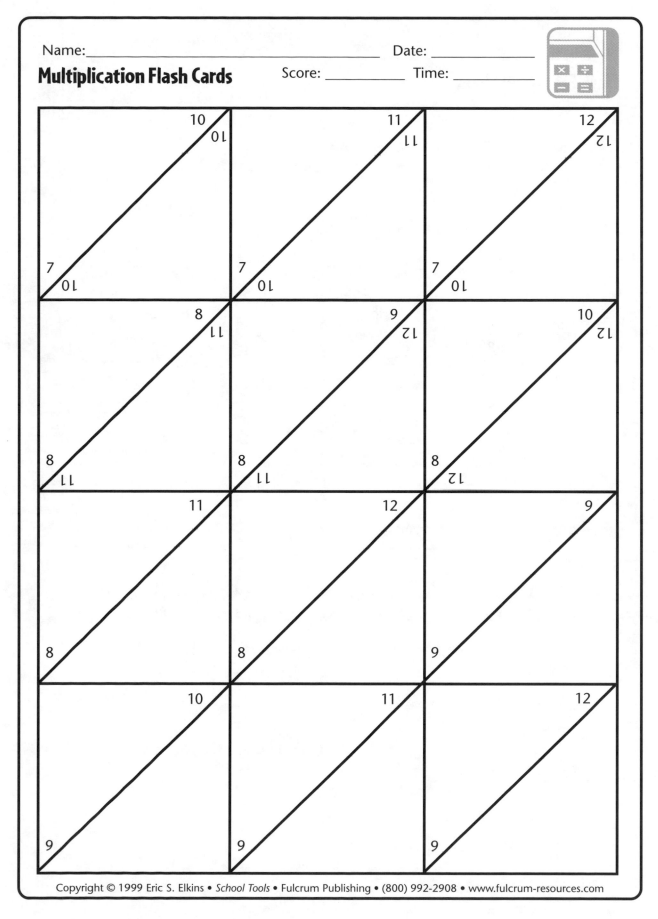

Name: _____ Date: _____

**Math Facts Drill Sheet**

Score: _____

Time: _____

| | | |
|---|---|---|
| 3 | 5 | 4 |
| x2 | x4 | x3 |

| | | | | | | |
|---|---|---|---|---|---|---|
| 4 | 6 | 8 | 9 | 5 | 3 | 2 |
| x5 | x6 | x7 | x3 | x6 | x6 | x1 |

| | | | | | | |
|---|---|---|---|---|---|---|
| 12 | 10 | 8 | 6 | 4 | 7 | 2 |
| x4 | x8 | x6 | x9 | x6 | x4 | x1 |

| | | | | | | |
|---|---|---|---|---|---|---|
| 11 | 3 | 12 | 7 | 5 | 4 | 2 |
| x11 | x2 | x10 | x4 | x2 | x2 | x2 |

| | | | | | | |
|---|---|---|---|---|---|---|
| 8 | 5 | 7 | 6 | 9 | 2 | 12 |
| x8 | x3 | x5 | x3 | x5 | x1 | x11 |

| | | | | | | |
|---|---|---|---|---|---|---|
| 2 | 9 | 7 | 5 | 10 | 8 | 4 |
| x4 | x6 | x5 | x2 | x3 | x4 | x3 |

| | | | | | | |
|---|---|---|---|---|---|---|
| 1 | 3 | 5 | 8 | 4 | 2 | 9 |
| x5 | x2 | x3 | x4 | x2 | x2 | x9 |

| | | | | |
|---|---|---|---|---|
| 5 | 9 | 7 | 1 | 12 |
| x4 | x8 | x6 | x1 | x12 |

Name:_____    Date: _____

**Math Facts Drill Sheet**                     Score: _____

                                               Time: _____

| | | | | | | |
|---|---|---|---|---|---|---|
| 9 | 8 | 7 | | | | |
| x2 | x4 | x3 | | | | |
| | | | | | | |
| 12 | 10 | 8 | 8 | 9 | 7 | 5 |
| x5 | x6 | x7 | x3 | x6 | x6 | x1 |
| | | | | | | |
| 8 | 9 | 9 | 7 | 5 | 4 | 6 |
| x4 | x8 | x6 | x9 | x6 | x4 | x1 |
| | | | | | | |
| 11 | 5 | 12 | 6 | 8 | 9 | 5 |
| x11 | x2 | x10 | x4 | x2 | x2 | x2 |
| | | | | | | |
| 9 | 6 | 8 | 12 | 5 | 4 | 12 |
| x8 | x3 | x5 | x3 | x5 | x1 | x11 |
| | | | | | | |
| 6 | 6 | 7 | 7 | 8 | 9 | 10 |
| x4 | x6 | x5 | x2 | x3 | x4 | x3 |
| | | | | | | |
| 9 | 8 | 9 | 7 | 4 | 9 | 12 |
| x5 | x2 | x3 | x4 | x2 | x2 | x9 |
| | | | | | | |
| 6 | 10 | 11 | 5 | 12 | | |
| x4 | x8 | x6 | x1 | x12 | | |

Name:_____    Date: _____

**Math Facts Drill Sheet**                Score: _____

                                          Time: _____

| | | |
|---|---|---|
| 9 | 8 | 7 |
| x4 | x6 | x7 |

| | | | | | | |
|---|---|---|---|---|---|---|
| 12 | 10 | 8 | 8 | 9 | 7 | 5 |
| x3 | x4 | x6 | x2 | x2 | x3 | x4 |

| | | | | | | |
|---|---|---|---|---|---|---|
| 8 | 9 | 9 | 7 | 5 | 4 | 6 |
| x5 | x6 | x7 | x7 | x2 | x2 | x2 |

| | | | | | | |
|---|---|---|---|---|---|---|
| 11 | 5 | 12 | 6 | 8 | 9 | 5 |
| x10 | x4 | x3 | x3 | x4 | x5 | x4 |

| | | | | | | |
|---|---|---|---|---|---|---|
| 9 | 6 | 8 | 12 | 5 | 4 | 12 |
| x2 | x3 | x3 | x9 | x4 | x2 | x7 |

| | | | | | | |
|---|---|---|---|---|---|---|
| 6 | 6 | 7 | 7 | 8 | 9 | 10 |
| x5 | x3 | x2 | x6 | x4 | x7 | x10 |

| | | | | | | |
|---|---|---|---|---|---|---|
| 9 | 8 | 9 | 7 | 4 | 9 | 12 |
| x2 | x4 | x5 | x3 | x3 | x6 | x5 |

| | | | | |
|---|---|---|---|---|
| 6 | 10 | 11 | 10 | 12 |
| x3 | x7 | x7 | x7 | x5 |

Name:_____ Date: _____

# Math Facts Flash Card Calendar

Your homework is to study your flash cards for at least ten minutes, five days each week.

| Sunday | Monday | Tuesday | Wednesday | Thursday | Friday | Saturday |
|---|---|---|---|---|---|---|
|  |  |  |  |  |  |  |

**Parents, please initial the days that your child practices for at least ten minutes.**

This slip is due: _____.

Parent Signature: _____

---

Name:_____ Date: _____

# Math Facts Flash Card Calendar

Your homework is to study your flash cards for at least ten minutes, five days each week.

| Sunday | Monday | Tuesday | Wednesday | Thursday | Friday | Saturday |
|---|---|---|---|---|---|---|
|  |  |  |  |  |  |  |

**Parents, please initial the days that your child practices for at least ten minutes.**

This slip is due: _____.

Parent Signature: _____

Name:_____ Date: _____

## Math Facts Tracking Sheet for _____

| Date: | Operation: | Goal: Time/Accuracy | | Time: | # Correct: |
|---|---|---|---|---|---|
| | | | | | |
| | | | | | |
| | | | | | |
| | | | | | |
| | | | | | |
| | | | | | |
| | | | | | |
| | | | | | |
| | | | | | |
| | | | | | |
| | | | | | |
| | | | | | |
| | | | | | |
| | | | | | |
| | | | | | |
| | | | | | |
| | | | | | |
| | | | | | |
| | | | | | |

# Math Problem-Solving Reports

**Purpose:**  To give students practice in writing clear explanations of the processes they use for solving problems.

**Process:**  Students are given a format to follow and are assigned a choice of two problems to solve.

**Payoff:**  Students are able to write detailed reports of how they solved long-term mathematics problems.

**Phases:**  All (depending on student ability)

## Standards Addressed

### *English Language Arts*

3. Students apply a wide range of strategies to comprehend, interpret, evaluate, and appreciate texts

4. Students adjust their use of spoken, written, and visual language (e.g., conventions, style, vocabulary) to communicate effectively with a variety of audiences for a variety of purposes.

### *Mathematics*

4. Mathematical Power
5. Problem Solving
6. Communication
8. Mathematical Concepts
9. Mathematical Procedures
10. Mathematical Disposition

## Materials needed

**Students Need:**  "Mathematics Problem Report Format" sheets (double sided, see page 83), paper, pencils, calculators

## Steps

1. Facilitate a discussion with students about why it would be useful to clearly explain how one solved a long-term problem. Eventually, relate the discussion to why sharing one's reasoning in a math problem could be useful. Don't forget to let your students know that a big reason is for them to demonstrate their understanding to you!

2. Explain that you will be introducing a new format for sharing the problem-solving process, by giving the students a choice of two problems to solve and asking them to write a short report explaining how they found their answers.

3. Distribute the format sheets and explain them.

*The Problem* is a personalized restatement of what the problem is that the student must solve. Included in this paragraph is an explanation of what information will be included in the solution.

*Considerations* is a paragraph about resources the student will need to solve the problem. This could include needing to go get prices, calling someone for information, and so forth.

*Calculations* are labeled to show what every number used in figuring out the solutions means.

*Solutions* answers the questions asked in The Problem. It is the "answer" to the problem being solved.

*Conclusion* analyzes the process of solving the problem. In this section the student discusses what difficulties occurred, how to make the process easier, what the student learned, and so forth.

4. Give students several days to work through this process.

## Extensions and Modifications

Although a few students may need prescriptive, step-by-step assistance, many will become excited by the freedom this project allows. Encourage students to make their problems more or less complex, depending on ability. My students are thrilled when solving their problems involves phone calls to businesses, research into costs, and so forth. Alternatively, students can create their own problems, solve them, and write the reports as instructed.

Name:_____  Date: _____

# Mathematics Problem Report Format

Your mathematics problem report will be a polished project. Each of the following should be a separate, neatly written section of the report.

I.  *The Problem*:       State exactly what the problem is and what you will be including in the solution.

II. *Considerations*:   What kinds of things will you need to figure out? What information will you need, where will you get it?

III. *Calculations*:      Show all of your math, labeling what each number means.

IV. *Solutions*:          Refer back to what you said you'd solve in *The Problem*. Clearly discuss all points of your solution and explain how you found your answers.

V. *Conclusion*:        What did you learn? How could you simplify the problem? What's another way to solve it?

**Problem A:** Plan a trip by car from our city to anywhere in the United States and back. You must give a complete itinerary, including total distance traveled, time needed, and total cost of the journey. Be certain to consider all expenses from food to fuel to lodging, and anything else you may want or need to purchase. Your trip must be realistic, practical, and at least a 1,000–mile round trip. There are no cost limitations. Obviously, you will need to research some of these costs.

**Problem B:** Plan a feast for at least 16 people, that includes a minimum of one appetizer, a salad, a main course, and a dessert. You must choose what foods to serve and submit recipes for each dish (these must be large enough to feed all of your guests; please include any changes you've made to the recipes to do this). You also must calculate the cost of each dish, other possible expenses, the total cost of the meal, and the total time required to prepare it.

*Jordana Arends*
*Math*

### The Problem

I need to do the interior of my barn. I need stalls, mats, and grills. I will need to figure out the cost of all of them to add it up. Then I have to worry about who will build it and how I have to pay.

### Considerations

Some things I will have to take into consideration is, I will need to figure out how much shipping of all this stuff costs. I will have to worry about where I will get my supplies from, and if they're good quality. Also if they're big enough, and if they're safe. Most of my information will be coming from catalogs and other places that are popular, so I know the quality of the supplies I am getting.

### Calculations

10 fronts=$2,689.50
8 dividers with bars=$1,494.16
14 dividers with no bars=$1,830.36
72 stall mats=$2,804.40

-----------------------------------------------------------------

72 Stall Mats—10 12'x12' stalls, and one washroom and an office (6 mats pr. stall)
12 stalls 72 stall mats
x 6 mats pr. stall x 38.95 price of mats
72 total mats needed $2,804.50 total price of mats

-----------------------------------------------------------------

10 fronts for 10 stalls
12 stalls $268.95 price of fronts
x 1 on front pr. stall x 10 total fronts
10 total fronts needed $2,689.50

-----------------------------------------------------------------

8 dividers with the bars—total # of dividers with bars, 2 stalls per divider
186.77 price of divider
x 8 # of dividers needed
$1,494.16
14 solid dividers (got by counting off the plans)
130.74 price of dividers
x 14 # of dividers
$1,830.36 total cost

### Solution

I got my answers from Stockyards. I didn't need to figure out delivery because my dad would do it. In my barn I will have 10 12'x12' feet stalls, one 12'x12' office, and one 12'x12' washroom. I got grills for the whole thing and mats for the whole thing. I don't need water right now, and the electricity isn't hooked up yet.

### Conclusion

I learned that even stuff that looks really easy to add isn't so easy. You could make it easier by calling the places and getting the prices, but then you would have to figure it out anyway.

### Kelsey Miller

### The Problem

I will be building a four bed, three bath, living room, kitchen, and family room, two story house. In my solution I will include the time it will take to build, the amount the house will cost, the type of landscape, the amount of paint, wood and carpet. I will also need to decide where the light fixtures, plug-ins, switches, doors, fire place, stairs, and windows will go. I will also decide how big each room will be, where the doors and windows in the room will be placed.

### Considerations

To make this a "good" project I will need to figure out about how much time it will take me to build my house, the cost, how much land I will need. I will find information from the yellow pages to help me with the cost.

### Calculation

(see pages 1–11)

### Solution

First of all, the total amount of the house is $30,009.78. I figured that the time it will take to build my house is one year. To find the cost of my house, first I go to Homebase and write down prices. Then on most prices I had to multiply to get the total cost (3X $15.10). Some I had to do 2 or 3 steps to get the answer. I found out how big the walls were going to be by drawing them, then measuring them by inches then converting inches to feet, then making them into hundreds.

## *Conclusion*

The first thing I learned was that building a house is hard. It takes time, effort, and money (even if you're doing the interior). The only way I can simplify this is in one word—hard. A house is very hard to build, and you have to be very precise (if you don't notice, the top floor would be bigger than the bottom). Another way I could have solved it was that I could have used different types of measurement. I also learned that you should respect the people who make houses because they put a lot of effort into making a house. They also have to use a lot of math.

## Chapter 4
# Social Studies and Language Arts Lessons

## Introduction

Cause and effect relationships help students to understand historical events. Because social studies can be an exercise in abstract perceptions of our past, students need mental structures for organizing their understanding. Placing historical, cultural, and personal events into the context of cause and effect relationships allows students to make sense of the world around them. Just as understanding the chronology of events helps students to develop a mental timeline of what has occurred, cause and effect recognition helps students develop mental charts that relate occurrences through causal events chains.

One of the reasons students are able to use this tool quickly is its intuitive nature. They see how cause and effect works all around them. Causal relationships occur around them every day. Students know that every decision they make has consequences, some predictable, some unforeseeable. I constantly remind my students that the choices they make have effects on the world around them. They know that tackling their little brothers will generally get them into some sort of trouble. They also know that, if they don't turn in their homework, they'll stay in from recess to complete it. The latter result is an effect, the cause of which was the decision to watch the latest episode of some insipid sitcom the night before. Students know that events in their lives occurred because of certain previous events. History makes more sense to students when they can place it into this context.

The primary purpose of many lessons in this chapter is to develop the recognition and language of cause and effect relationships. By starting to use this cognitive organizer at the beginning of the year and consistently expanding on its utility, students will place it in their minds as a tool that works.

As the school year progresses, students will begin to refer to the consequences of misbehavior as cause and effect relationships. They will say, "The cause is, I ran down the hall, the effect is, I have to go back and walk." They'll begin to see their responsibility on both sides of the equation. Encourage students to see that the effects of certain causes can be controlled by

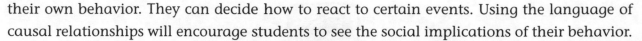
their own behavior. They can decide how to react to certain events. Using the language of causal relationships will encourage students to see the social implications of their behavior.

As students become comfortable with the idea of simple cause and effect trains, more complex concepts, such as the difference between "physical" and "emotional" causal relationships, will become useful. A physical cause tends to have predictable effects. It relies more on concrete events. I leave my mug of putrid teacher's lounge coffee on my desk for several days; it becomes a science experiment of unidentifiable goo. On the other hand, some unpredictable emotional effects result from some causes (I accidentally drink the moldy coffee, like it, and make more), and we may not be able figure out the causes of some "emotional" effects. ("Tell me about your childhood" doesn't always give us the answers.) Emotional cause and effect relationships tend to be more complicated than physical ones, because there are more unseen influences on both sides of the event.

# Cause and Effect Game

**Purpose:** To introduce the importance of recognizing cause and effect relationships.

**Process:** The teacher and students describe a hypothetical or historical event and follow several effect pathways the event caused.

**Payoff:** Students understand, then demonstrate, the ability to identify cause and effect relationships.

**Phase:** Introduction

## Standards Addressed
### *National Center for History in the Schools: Historical Thinking*

Standard 1. Chronological Thinking

    A. Distinguish between past, present, and future time.

    B. Identify in historical narratives the temporal structure of a historical narrative or story.

    C. Establish temporal order in constructing historical narratives of their own.

Standard 3. Historical Analysis and Interpretation

    E. Analyze cause-and-effect relationships and multiple causation, including the importance of the individual, the influence of ideas, and the role of chance.

    J. Hypothesize the influence of the past.

Standard 5. Historical Issues–Analysis and Decision–Making

    B. Marshal evidence of antecedent circumstances and contemporary factors contributing to problems and alternative courses of action.

    C. Identify relevant historical antecedents.

    D. Evaluate alternative courses of action.

### *Social Studies*

2. Time, Continuity and Change: Social studies programs should include experiences that provide for the study of the ways human beings view themselves in and over time.

## Materials Needed

No materials needed.

## Steps

1. To start the game, explain that all events have causes and effects. Drop a pencil on the floor and discuss some physical causes and effects. Physical causes and effects can often be predicted. They are usually observable. A cause could be that the pencil was slippery. An effect could be that the point breaks, the pencil makes a noise, and so forth.

2. Next, discuss possible emotional causes and effects of the pencil drop. Emotional causes and effects are not usually predictable and are not always observable. They may not come to light immediately, sometimes taking time to develop. Physical causes can lead to emotional and physical effects, and emotional causes (which are often emotions, like anger) can lead to physical effects. So, if you were startled (emotional), you may have dropped the pencil (physical). Or, the pencil slipped out of your hand (physical) and made you frustrated (emotional).

3. Describe a physical event. I like to use: A child throws a rock into a pond. Ask students to raise their hands with some possible effects of this cause. Follow a single pathway at a time, then go back to the original event and follow other pathways. Do this with other possible causes (have students propose some). Help students recognize how effects can become causes and point out the differences and similarities of emotional and physical cause and effect relationships.

4. Describe some appropriate historical events and discuss the cause and effect relationships.

5. This game should be played throughout the School Tools unit to assess understanding and ability.

## Extensions and Modifications

Some students may wish to draw cause and effect flow charts so they can actually see how the chain of events could take place. Very concrete, physical causes and effects are often the best way to start, so students can make logical predictions.

# Cause and Effect Video

**Purpose:** To give students practice in recognizing cause and effect relationships.

**Process:** The teacher and students watch a video, keeping track of causes and effects.

**Payoff:** Students continue to identify cause and effect relationships.

**Phase:** Guided Practice

## Standards Addressed

### *National Center for History in the Schools: Historical Thinking*

Standard 1. Chronological Thinking

    A. Distinguish between past, present, and future time.

    B. Identify in historical narratives the temporal structure of a historical narrative or story.

    C. Establish temporal order in constructing historical narratives of their own.

Standard 3. Historical Analysis and Interpretation

    E. Analyze cause-and-effect relationships and multiple causation, including the importance of the individual, the influence of ideas, and the role of chance.

    J. Hypothesize the influence of the past.

Standard 5. Historical Issues–Analysis and Decision–Making

    B. Marshal evidence of antecedent circumstances and contemporary factors contributing to problems and alternative courses of action.

    C. Identify relevant historical antecedents.

    D. Evaluate alternative courses of action.

### *Social Studies*

    2. Time, Continuity and Change: Social studies programs should include experiences that provide for the study of the ways human beings view themselves in and over time.

## Materials Needed

**Students Need:** Personal journals or paper, pencils

**Teacher Needs:** VCR/TV, a short film or video (I use *The Wrong Trousers*, a stop-action film from BBC). Some other possibilities are:

    • *A Grand Day Out* or *A Close Shave* (also from BBC)

    • Any of the Eyewitness Videos (by DK Visions), such as *Dinosaur* and *Seashore*, or other nature/environment videos

    • The Bill Nye videos (by Disney)

    • The Wishbone videos (by PBS), also excellent.

## Steps

1. Inform students that they will be watching a short feature and will have to list as many cause and effect relationships as they can.

2. Have students divide their papers into two columns, "Cause" and "Effect."

3. Watch the film, encouraging students to write down causes and subsequent effects in their respective columns.

4. After the film, launch a discussion on what the students listed. Distinctions between physical and emotional causes and effects will be valuable during this discussion.

## Extensions and Modifications

Because students will be interested in the video, some may wish to merely write one word notes, rather than complete thoughts. If you wish, be ready with the "pause" button, to stop, rewind, and draw attention to certain causal relationships in the program you are watching.

# Cause and Effect Personal Essay Assessment

**Purpose:** To give students a chance to apply the organization of causal relationships to their personal growth and development.

**Process:** Students write an essay.

**Payoff:** Students apply what they have learned about cause and effect relationships.

**Phases:** Application, Risk

## Standards Addressed

### *English Language Arts*

4. Students adjust their use of spoken, written, and visual language (e.g., conventions, style, vocabulary) to communicate effectively with a variety of audiences for a variety of purposes.

5. Students apply knowledge of language structure, language conventions (e.g., spelling and punctuation), media techniques, figurative language, and genre to create, critique, and discuss print and nonprint texts.

12. Students use spoken, written, and visual language to accomplish their own purposes (e.g., for learning, enjoyment, persuasion, and the exchange of information).

### *National Center for History in the Schools: Historical Thinking*

Standard 1. Chronological Thinking

A. Distinguish between past, present, and future time.

Standard 3: Historical Analysis and Interpretation

E. Analyze cause-and-effect relationships and multiple causation, including the importance of the individual, the influence of ideas, and the role of chance.

J. Hypothesize the influence of the past.

Standard 5. Historical Issues–Analysis and Decision–Making

B. Marshal evidence of antecedent circumstances and contemporary factors contributing to problems and alternative courses of action.

C. Identify relevant historical antecedents.

D. Evaluate alternative courses of action.

### *Social Studies*

2. Time, Continuity and Change: Social studies programs should include experiences that provide for the study of the ways human beings view themselves in and over time.

4. Individual Development and Identity: Social studies programs should include experiences that provide for the study of individual development and identity.

5. Individuals, Groups and Institutions: Social studies programs should include experiences that provide for the study of interactions among individuals, groups, and institutions.

## Materials Needed

**Students Need:**   Notebook paper, pencils

## Steps

1. Ask students to list and describe several examples of physical and emotional cause and effect relationships in their lives. You may ask them to write this in essay format.

## Extensions and Modifications

Certain students may do better in an interview situation. Use questions or statements such as:

What are cause and effect relationships?

Describe a cause and effect relationship at home.

Would you say that is a physical or emotional causal relationship?

Describe a cause and effect relationship at school.

How are consequences like effects?

How is your behavior like a cause?

Some students may wish to draw cause and effect relationship flow charts, rather than write an essay.

## *Cause and Effect Essay*
## *By Blair Harp*

Physical and emotional causes and effects are tied together in almost every way. Emotional causes and effects are everywhere. Physical causes and effects are also a big part of my life.

Physical causes and effects are a huge part of me, and affect me in every way. When I fight with my brothers, I get bruises and cuts. In sports, physical causes and effects are huge. If I hit the ball, I run around the bases, but that's a simple one. In football, if I don't stay low, I can get hurt or ruin the play for the team. School has lots of physical causes and effects, like when I get paper cuts, they lead to pain and a band-aid.

Emotional causes and effects are everywhere. In school, there are lots of emotional causes and effects. Like when I can't figure something out and I feel frustrated. Or when you try to learn something, but it just doesn't make sense. When I fight with my brother, I get in trouble, I feel sad, then mad, then I go to my room to get over it. Sports are a huge part of emotional causes and effects, like when I feel pain and get frustrated because I know I could have done better.

Physical and emotional causes and effects are often tied together. Like in sports when I get a goal I feel happy and I get cheered on by my team. Or in school when I do something bad I don't feel good inside and I'm getting in trouble. Physical causes and effects are always there and there is nothing anyone can do about them. That is the same with emotional causes and effects.

# Cause and Effect in Social Studies

The next step is to remind students to look for cause and effect relationships in whatever content they learn for the rest of the year. By organizing many lectures, assignments, and assessments into a cause and effect structure, you will encourage students to find these patterns and to move into the Application and Risk phases of the School Tools learning process.

In teaching the conflicts of the twentieth century, we provided the students with many opportunities to learn about each conflict. We gave lectures, facilitated activities, screened videos, and provided a mix of media materials for each conflict. Several times, our class's daily perusal of the newspaper paid off in related articles. As a class, we defined different types of causes and effects. For instance, students discerned economic, social, and political dimensions. Next, students were required to create "Century Books," where, for every conflict, they made at least one page on political, economic, and social causes; one page on political, economic, and social effects; and one creative page.

We used these books to discern patterns in twentieth-century conflict. By the end of the unit, students had "discovered" many causes and effects in common across the decades. At the end, we used a news story I heard on National Public Radio to create a potential world crisis. The students were required to write a fictional chronology and list of causes and effects of a conflict arising from the conditions described. We were quite pleased when students applied their knowledge to describe causes and effects that were very much like the real conflicts of the twentieth century. A sample of the test, as well as examples of student work from the unit, follow.

*Kelsey Miller*
*The Great Depression*

## Causes

**Nobody needed crops**

S—Farmers started depression before every one else.

E—It cost more money to grow crops than to sell crops.

Germany had no money

E—Well it's obvious, they had no money.

S—Many people suffered.

P—It made Germany vulnerable to Adolf Hitler.

People not buying stocks

E—It cost money for people and banks.

S—Well you know the saying, monkey see, monkey do.

Americans won't buy from Europe

E—Can't pay Americans back for loans.

P—Hoover says "We can survive."

S—People were suffering.

## Effects

**FDR runs against "do nothing" Hoover**

S—Everybody hates Hoover.

P—FDR won the election.

E—Cost money to debate.

New deal for Americans

E—Cost money, but was worth it.

S—Saved people jobs and money.

P—Congress was happy.

Movies started

S—Shirley Temple started.

E—Only a nickel to see.

Name:_____     Date: _____

# An Assessment on Conflict

On a small island called Cyprus, in the Mediterranean Sea, the citizens are preparing for possible conflict. You see, the island is divided between Greek Cypriots and Turkish Cypriots (a Cypriot is someone who lives on Cyprus), and they don't get along. Both sides have been buying weapons from the United States and Russia. Yes, they are escalating the technology of their guns and fighter planes.

   Also, the governments of Turkey and Greece are in alliance with their people in Cyprus! That means that Turkey will back up the Turkish side of the island, and Greece will back up the Greek side. Both Turkey and Greece are part of NATO, but relations between Turkey and the U.S. have been somewhat strained lately. What do you think will happen?

**Your assignment:**
Emergency! War has been declared on the island of Cyprus! Assume a war has been fought. Using what you know about conflicts in the twentieth century, do the following:
   First, make up a chronology of the conflict. For instance:

   September 4: Turkish Cypriots start burning Greek Cypriots' homes.
   September 6: etc.
   (Provide at least 10 events in the conflict)

   Second, create cause and effect sheets (with Social, Political, and Economic reasons) for your made-up war. Provide at least three causes and three long-term effects of this war. This should be a list, with reasons why each cause or effect is social, political, and/or economic.

Your work will be graded by looking at how you used your knowledge of conflict to create a war that could really happen. We will look for events that other conflicts had in common and accurate causes and effects (things that could really happen in a twentieth-century conflict).

# Chapter 5
# Science Lessons

# Introduction

## Inquiry as a Process
## (or "Yet Another Format to Learn")

I have several "scientists" in my classroom. They are the kids who have to touch, smell, or even taste new stimuli in their environments, they are the ones who wander off when we're on field trips to investigate something new and exciting. My scientists are inquisitive and curious and require non-stop vigilance. If only all students were so intensely observant!

The scientific process that students learn in these lessons will help them to classify their observations and do experiments in a controlled manner. Once they get the format down (as in all of the School Tools), they will be able to use their proficiency in designing their experiments.

The following lesson plans fall into two categories: observation and experiment. In an experiment, the students perform certain tasks after formulating a hypothesis of what will happen. The primary action in an observation is done by the teacher while the students watch. They do not hypothesize, they watch (and listen and smell) carefully and write or draw what they observe. The observations in this book serve the purpose of encouraging students to be specific in their attempts to gather data, while giving them practice in using the scientific inquiry process. Experiments allow them to truly use the process.

Understanding cause and effect relationships is essential to developing a mental framework for the scientific process. Therefore, be sure to accent the causal relationships in each lesson.

# Introduction to the Scientific Process

**Purpose:** To introduce students to a specific format to use in the recording of scientific investigation.

**Process:** Students receive a template to glue into their science notebooks and use the template in a prescriptive experiment.

**Payoff:** Students practice a procedure they will be using throughout the year (and in the future).

**Phase:** Introduction

## Standards Addressed

### *Science*

A. As a result of activities in grades 5–8, all students should develop abilities necessary to do scientific inquiry.

G. As a result of activities in grades 5–8, all students should develop understanding of science as a human endeavor, nature of science, history of science.

## Materials Needed

**Students Need:** A "Proper Format" sheet (see page 100), spiral notebook, pencils, glue

**Teacher Needs:** 200 paper clips, clear glass or beaker filled to the top with water, some paper towels (just in case), work space where all students can see the demonstration

## Steps

1. Explain to students that from now on they will be conducting scientific investigations and writing about their work in a very specific format. Generate a discussion on why it might be important for people to use a recognizable format in science. Look for ideas about replicating experiments for validity and reliability, being able to understand someone else's work and build off of it, and so forth.

2. Pass out sheets and have students glue them into the front covers of their spiral notebooks. Go through each element of the template, explaining that this format will be followed for all pursuits. Have students leave the first page of their notebooks blank to use as a table of contents.

3. Have students write the date and title for today's experiment in the proper locations on the next page. Write the title "Clip and Save" on the board.

4. Next, have students write "Purpose:" then the following in their notebooks, "To observe an experiment and practice proper scientific steps." Explain that this experiment will be done to give students a chance to try out the new format.

5. Have students write "Hypothesis:" in their notebooks and explain that a hypothesis is a prediction or guess about what will happen. Explain that you will be placing paper

clips in a beaker full of water until it overflows and that, in this case, each student's hypothesis will be, "The number of paper clips that will go into the water before it overflows is __." Students fill in their own predictions.

6. Write the steps listed below on the board for the students.

## Materials Needed

Paper clips, water, beaker, paper towels

## Steps

1. Fill a beaker to top with tap water.
2. Place beaker on a flat surface.
3. Gently drop paper clips into water until beaker overflows.
4. Keep track of number of paper clips used.
7. Have students write "Procedure:" and copy it down.
8. Have students write "Data and Observations:" in their notebooks. Instruct them to write hash marks for the number of paper clips you drop in and to document any other observations they have.
9. When students are ready, begin the experiment. Make sure students are keeping track of your paper clips.
10. When the beaker finally overflows, have students write down the number and circle it in their notebooks.
11. Ask students to write "Analysis:" and their explanations for what they observed. You may wish to encourage them to write down new questions this experiment raised for them and possible follow-up experiments to answer the new questions. Explain that this is the scientific cycle.
12. For conclusion, have students write "Conclusion: My hypothesis was _____." (correct or incorrect).

## Extensions and Modifications

Strips of paper, on which headings from the "Proper Format" sheets have been copied could be glued into notebooks each time a new experiment or observation is done, if students are having trouble writing them in. Also, copying the procedures and having students glue them in would save time.

Name:_____  Date: _____

# Proper Format for Your Science Journal Entries

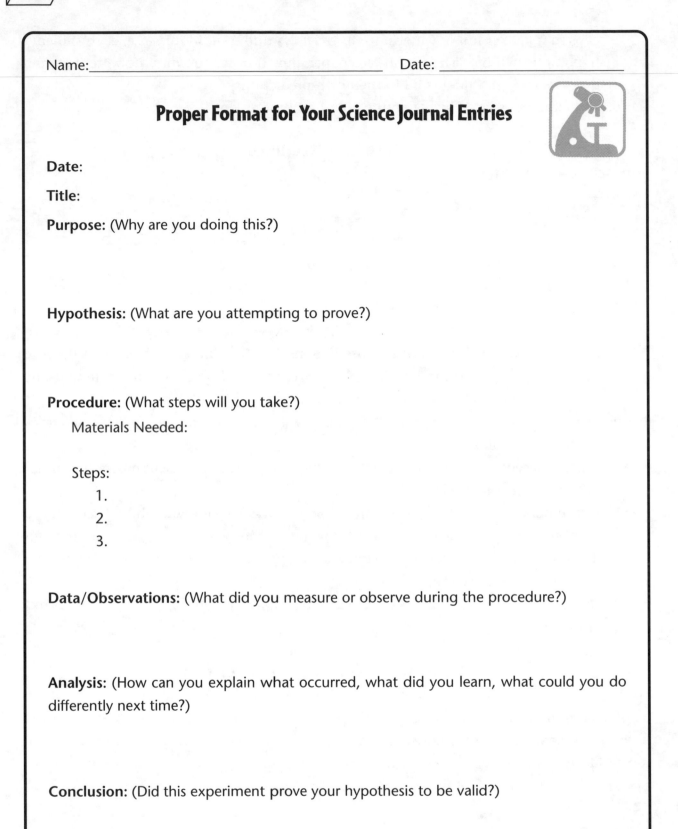

**Date:**

**Title:**

**Purpose:** (Why are you doing this?)



**Hypothesis:** (What are you attempting to prove?)



**Procedure:** (What steps will you take?)

    Materials Needed:

    Steps:

        1.

        2.

        3.

**Data/Observations:** (What did you measure or observe during the procedure?)



**Analysis:** (How can you explain what occurred, what did you learn, what could you do differently next time?)



**Conclusion:** (Did this experiment prove your hypothesis to be valid?)

# Observation #1:
# Potato Candle

**Purpose:** To give students a chance to question their own observation skills and assumptions.

**Process:** Students watch the teacher light what appears to be a candle and document their observations.

**Payoff:** Students learn that seeing is not always believing.

**Phase:** Introduction

## Standards Addressed

### *Science*

A. As a result of activities in grades 5–8, all students should develop abilities necessary to do scientific inquiry.

G. As a result of activities in grades 5–8, all students should develop understanding of science as a human endeavor, nature of science, history of science.

## Materials Needed

**Students Need:** Science notebooks, pencils

**Teacher Needs:** A potato candle (potato, string, candle), matches, a small tin or a candle holder that fits

## Steps

1. In advance, peel a potato until it looks like a household candle. Blanch it in boiling water for three or four minutes, so it won't brown. Cut a small piece of string, to look like a wick. Light a candle and drip a small drop of wax onto the string (so it will burn properly). Place the "wick" into a hole in the top of the potato.

2. In the classroom, ask students to write the following in their notebooks:

   **Date:**

   **Observation #1** (title):

   **Purpose:** To test my observation skills.

   **Hypothesis:** None (Explain that because this is an observation and not an experiment, the students will not have a hypothesis for it.)

   **Procedure:**

   **Materials Needed:** None

   **Steps:**

   > 1. Observe teacher's actions.
   > 2. Write down all observations in journal.

   **Data/Observations:**

3. Place "candle" in holder on tin or holder.

4. Light "wick"; immediately blow it out. Repeat.

5. Remind students to write down all of their observations and give them time to do so.

6. Have some students share their observations (if this goes really well, several students will use the words "candle" and "wick").

7. Show students that what you really set on fire was a potato. (If you're feeling really daring, take a bite of it!) Ask students if their observations were truly accurate, or if they made assumptions about what they saw. Stress the importance of accurate observation, writing only what can be measured or proven.

8. Under "Analysis," ask students to write what they learned from this activity. Don't get too upset if they write something about you being a big fat cheater!

9. Under "Conclusion," have them write, "None," because there was no hypothesis.

## Extensions and Modifications

Strips of paper, on which headings from the "Proper Format" sheets have been copied could be glued into notebooks each time a new experiment or observation is done, if students are having trouble writing them in. Also, copying the procedures and having students glue them in would save time.

# Observation #2:
# Matchless

**Purpose:** To give students another chance to question their own observation skills and assumptions.

**Process:** Students watch the teacher play with matchboxes.

**Payoff:** Students learn, yet again, that seeing (and hearing) is not always believing.

**Phase:** Guided Practice

## Standards Addressed

### Science

A. As a result of activities in grades 5–8, all students should develop abilities necessary to do scientific inquiry.

G. As a result of activities in grades 5–8, all students should develop understanding of science as a human endeavor, nature of science, history of science.

## Materials Needed

**Students Need:** Science notebooks, pencils

**Teacher Needs:** Four identical matchboxes, one of which is full, the others empty, masking tape, one rubber band, a long-sleeved shirt

## Steps

1. In advance, empty matches out of three boxes and conspicuously tape them closed. Fill the last box with enough matches to make a convincing rattling sound when shaken. Attach the box with the matches to your right wrist (under your sleeve) with a rubber band (don't let it shake too much or you'll be given away). Try this trick a few times before you do it in front of the class.

2. In the classroom, ask students to write the following in their notebooks:

   **Date:**

   **Observation #2** (title):

   **Purpose:** To test my observation skills again.

   **Hypothesis:** None (Explain that because this is an observation and not an experiment, the students will not have a hypothesis for it.)

   **Procedure:**

   **Materials Needed:** None

   **Steps**

      1. Observe teacher's actions

      2. Write down all observations in journal.

   **Data/Observations:**

3. Place three empty boxes side by side on the table. Say something about having three boxes in front of you (find a "patter" that works).

4. Pick up the middle box with your right hand and shake it, ostensibly showing that it is full of matches. Shake the other two boxes with your left hand to show that they are empty.

5. Have students watch carefully as you move the center box (kind of a slow-motion version of three-card monte). After you have very obviously moved the box around, have them pick the box that has the matches in it. Show them that they are correct by shaking the selected box with your right hand. Shake the others with your left hand. Do this a few times, giving them false confidence in their powers of observation.

6. Then, do a very obvious scramble and, after they have picked the box, shake it with your left hand (gasp!). Shake another with your left hand and, finally, the last with your right hand. Fool them a few times before you escalate the wonder.

7. Next, "pull" the matches out of one box and "put" them into another. Shake the new box with your right hand (double gasp!). Move them around like that once or twice, then move some matches into all of the boxes and shake each one, in turn, with your right hand (triple gasp!).

8. Finally, "pull" all of the matches out of the boxes and shake them with your left hand. ... They're gone (quadruple gasp)!

9. Admonish the spellbound students to write down their observations.

10. At this point, you may wish to show them "the trick" to find out if anyone wrote down with which hand you shook the boxes.

11. For "Analysis," ask them to write down what they learned, in addition to the obvious, "Our teacher is tricky."

12. Under "Conclusion," have them write "None," because there was no hypothesis.

## Extensions and Modifications

Strips of paper, on which headings from the "Proper Format" sheets have been copied could be glued into notebooks each time a new experiment or observation is done, if students are having trouble writing them in. Also, copying the procedures and having students glue them in would save time.

# Causal Relationships #1: Balloon on Flask

**Purpose:** To show how the recognition of cause and effect relationships is helpful in scientific investigation.

**Process:** Students watch what happens when the teacher places a balloon over the mouth of a cold flask or bottle.

**Payoff:** Students begin explaining phenomena in terms of cause and effect, while practicing their use of scientific inquiry.

**Phase:** Exercise

## Standards Addressed

### *Science*

A. As a result of activities in grades 5–8, all students should develop abilities necessary to do scientific inquiry.

B. As a result of their activities in grades 5–8, all students should develop an understanding of properties and changes of properties in matter, motions and forces, transfer of energy.

G. As a result of activities in grades 5–8, all students should develop understanding of science as a human endeavor, nature of science, history of science.

### *National Center for History in the Schools: Historical Thinking*

Standard 3. Historical Analysis and Interpretation

E. Analyze cause-and-effect relationships and multiple causation, including the importance of the individual, the influence of ideas, and the role of chance.

## Materials Needed

**Students Need:** Science notebooks, pencils

**Teacher Needs:** A balloon (or one for every pair or small group of students, if desired), a freezing-cold flask or glass bottle (or one for every pair or small group of students, if desired)

## Steps

1. Have students set up their notebooks with the following:

   **Date:**

   **Cause and Effect #1: Balloon and Flask** (title):

   **Purpose:** To practice recognizing physical cause and effect relationships.

   **Hypothesis:** (Leave blank until procedure is written, then have students write down what they think will happen)

**Procedure:**

**Materials Needed:**

    A freezing cold ____

    A balloon

**Steps**

    1. Place the balloon over the mouth of the ___.

    2. Write down all observations in your journal.

**Data/Observations:**

2. Pull bottle or flask out of the freezer at the very last minute and immediately place the balloon over its mouth. As the flask warms up, it should slowly inflate the balloon. Encourage students to write down their observations (depending on your preferences, you could have them keep track of the time of each observation as well).

3. Have students write down their analyses of why they think what occurred and some questions raised by the experiment. Be sure to have students write their analyses in terms of the possible causes for the observed effects on the balloon.

4. Have them write under "Conclusion" whether their hypotheses were correct or incorrect.

5. Optional: Assign students the homework of designing an experiment, which could be done in class, to prove their current analysis. From there, you may wish to pursue this path, allowing students to work in small groups to design new experiments. Ensure that each student follows the proper notebook format before allowing him or her to conduct the experiment.

## Extensions and Modifications

Strips of paper, on which headings from the "Proper Format" sheets have been copied could be glued into notebooks each time a new experiment or observation is done, if students are having trouble writing them in. Also, copying the procedures and having students glue them in would save time.

# Causal Relationships #2:
# Imploding Can

**Purpose:** To continue study of physical cause and effect relationships in scientific investigation.

**Process:** Students watch what happens when the teacher heats an empty aluminum can and places it in cold water.

**Payoff:** Students attempt to explain phenomena in terms of cause and effect, while practicing their use of scientific inquiry.

**Phase:** Exercise

## Standards Addressed

### *National Center for History in the Schools: Historical Thinking*

Standard 3. Historical Analysis and Interpretation

    E. Analyze cause-and-effect relationships and multiple causation, including the importance of the individual, the influence of ideas, and the role of chance.

### *Science*

    A. As a result of activities in grades 5–8, all students should develop abilities necessary to do scientific inquiry.

    B. As a result of their activities in grades 5–8, all students should develop an understanding of properties and changes of properties in matter, motions and forces, transfer of energy.

    G. As a result of activities in grades 5–8, all students should develop understanding of science as a human endeavor, nature of science, history of science, historical thinking.

## Materials Needed

**Students Need:** Science notebooks, pencils

**Teacher Needs:** Some sort of heater or burner, an empty soda can, a tub of cold water, tongs

## Steps

1. Have students prepare their notebooks for the next experiment. The purpose will be, "To observe and explain a physical cause and effect relationship." After you describe the procedure, ask them to hypothesize what will happen in the experiment.

2. Place between two and five milliliters of water in the can.

3. Using tongs, hold the can over the heat until it is extremely hot (and the water is almost completely vaporized).

4. Quickly place the can, hole-end down, into the water. The can should crumple. You may wish to repeat the experiment with another can or two.

5. Have students write down their observations.

6. Ask students to write down their analyses of what happened, in terms of cause and effect. As the air in the can was heated, it became less dense. That is, the concentration of air inside the can became much less than the concentration of air outside the can. When the hole was sealed by placing the can in the water, the outside air attempted to get into the can, thereby crushing it in the process. The force of the outside (more concentrated) air caused the can to implode.

   Cause: Higher concentration of outside air

   Effect: Crushes the can like an elephant on a peanut.

7. Have students write about the accuracy of their hypotheses under "Conclusion."

## Extensions and Modifications

Strips of paper, on which headings from the "Proper Format" sheets have been copied could be glued into notebooks each time a new experiment or observation is done, if students are having trouble writing them in. Also, copying the procedures and having students glue them in would save time.

# Causal Relationships #3:
# Flying Balloons

**Purpose:** To further investigate physical cause and effect relationships while testing hypotheses.

**Process:** Students watch what happens when the teacher lets loose a blown-up balloon, then design experiments to prove their hypotheses.

**Payoff:** Students attempt to explain phenomena in terms of cause and effect, while practicing their use of scientific inquiry.

**Phase:** Exercise

## Standards Addressed

### *National Center for History in the School: Historical Thinking*

Standard 3. Historical Analysis and Interpretation

    E.  Analyze cause-and-effect relationships and multiple causation, including the importance of the individual, the influence of ideas, and the role of chance.

### *Science*

    A.  As a result of activities in grades 5–8, all students should develop abilities necessary to do scientific inquiry.

    B.  As a result of their activities in grades 5–8, all students should develop an understanding of properties and changes of properties in matter motions and forces, transfer of energy.

    G.  As a result of activities in grades 5–8, all students should develop understanding of science as a human endeavor; nature of science, history of science, historical thinking.

## Materials Needed

**Students Need:** Science journals, pencils, one balloon for every four students, one plastic freezer bag for every four students, one soda straw for every four students, string, tape

**Teacher Needs:** One balloon, patience

## Steps

1. In front of the students, blow up a balloon and let it go. Do it again. Ask the students not to divulge why they think the balloon did what it did.

2. Tell them that they must design and conduct an experiment to prove why they think the balloon behaved that way. Tell them that the only materials they can use are:

    A balloon

    A plastic sandwich bag

Two soda straws

String

Tape

Rubber bands

Masking tape

3. Divide the class into groups of four and instruct them to agree on an explanation, then design an experiment to prove it. Tell them that they will not receive the materials until their notebooks are filled out properly.

4. Make sure that student groups have convincing purposes, hypotheses, and procedures (exact length of string, and so forth) before giving them their materials.

5. Allow the students plenty of time to conduct their experiments, write down their data and observations, analyze their work, and conclude whether or not their hypotheses were correct.

6. Debrief students on how their experiments went. Be sure to address ideas of experimental design and inquiry, as well as causal relationships.

## Extensions and Modifications

This experiment can get loud and unruly without vigilance. Some students may need you to prompt them in finding an explanation for the balloon's behavior. Because this is a hands-on lesson, some students may not be able to plan their experiments on paper first. They might need to "play" with the materials for a few minutes before designing and writing up the experiment.

## Chapter 6
# Mid-Year Unit
### Review and Assess: Build a City

# Introduction

In this one-week unit, students are reintroduced to the School Tools in a concentrated way. While they create, design, and build a city, they use the tools learned at the beginning of the year. Hopefully, students have been encouraged to use these tools all year long. This integrated mini-unit provides a fun, interesting, and useful way to remind students of the utility of the School Tools, while giving you the opportunity to evaluate student abilities.

This unit is designed to include group and individual accountability. It will require some direct instruction; low-structure group work time; and quiet, individual work time. Feel free to incorporate regular, weekly activities and lessons into the plan (for example, spelling tests, silent reading time, and so forth). If necessary, this unit can be stretched over a two-week time span to allow for your other classroom routines.

# Lesson 1: Tale of a City

**Purpose:** To provide a context for the unit.

**Process:** With the teacher's help, students brainstorm what they know about their town, then try to tie cause and effect relationships to their knowledge.

**Payoff:** Students begin to get understand that a city is more than buildings.

### Standards Addressed
### *National Center for History in the Schools: Historical Thinking*
Standard 1. Chronological Thinking
  A. Distinguish between past, present, and future time.
  B. Identify in historical narratives the temporal structure of a historical narrative or story.
  C. Establish temporal order in constructing historical narratives of their own.

Standard 3. Historical Analysis and Interpretation

    E. Analyze cause-and-effect relationships and multiple causation, including the importance of the individual, the influence of ideas, and the role of chance.

    J. Hypothesize the influence of the past.

Standard 5. Historical Issues–Analysis and Decision–Making

    B. Marshal evidence of antecedent circumstances and contemporary factors contributing to problems and alternative courses of action.

    C. Identify relevant historical antecedents.

    D. Evaluate alternative courses of action.

## *Social Studies*

2. Time, Continuity and Change: Social studies programs should include experiences that provide for the study of the ways human beings view themselves in and over time.

5. Individuals, Groups and Institutions: Social studies programs should include experiences that provide for the study of interactions among individuals, groups, and institutions.

## *Geography*

The geographically informed person knows and understands:

12. The processes, patterns, and functions of human settlement.

## Materials Needed

**Teacher Needs:** Markers, butcher paper

## Steps

1. Inform students that they are beginning a unit of study that will allow them to review the School Tools and how they use them. Do a brief review by asking which of the Tools they remember and which they use nearly every day. Let the students know that part of this review will be a project, in which they create their own city.

2. Ask students to brainstorm what they know about their own city or town. Be sure to write down as much as possible and encourage them with questions such as:

    How is our city governed?

    Who is in charge?

    Is our city growing? Shrinking? Staying the same?

    How is our town organized?

    Are there any famous people from our area?

    What's special about our town?

    What's important about our town?

    What problems do we have in our city?

3.  After you have culled as much information as possible from the students, start a new piece of butcher paper, creating a cause and effect T–chart. Facilitate a cause and effect analysis of information students volunteered. For instance, you might write "More people are moving to our city" on the "Effect" side of the first line and ask students to brainstorm possible causes of this migration. Then write "More people are moving to our city" on the "Cause" side of the next line and generate possible effects of this development. Explain that a "cause and effect" analysis means looking at both sides (the causes and effects) of an issue. Complete an analysis for as many points as possible.

## Extensions and Modifications

Some students may wish to speak to their parents about some of the issues discussed. Encourage them to get "reality checks" on their cause and effect analyses. You may (if possible) want to take your students on a walking tour of the town.

# Lesson 2: Introduction of the Project

**Purpose:** To provide a structure for the project.

**Process:** Students receive a handout, outlining their responsibilities.

**Payoff:** Students begin designing their cities.

## Standards Addressed

### *English Language Arts*

4. Students adjust their use of spoken, written, and visual language (e.g., conventions, style, vocabulary) to communicate effectively with a variety of audiences for a variety of purposes.

5. Students apply knowledge of language structure, language conventions (e.g., spelling and punctuation), media techniques, figurative language, and genre to create, critique, and discuss print and nonprint texts.

12. Students use spoken, written, and visual language to accomplish their own purposes (e.g., for learning, enjoyment, persuasion, and the exchange of information).

### *National Center for History in the Schools: Historical Thinking*

Standard 1. Chronological Thinking

   A. Distinguish between past, present, and future time.

   B. Identify in historical narratives the temporal structure of a historical narrative or story.

   C. Establish temporal order in constructing historical narratives of their own.

Standard 3. Historical Analysis and Interpretation

   E. Analyze cause-and-effect relationships and multiple causation, including the importance of the individual, the influence of ideas, and the role of chance.

   J. Hypothesize the influence of the past.

Standard 5. Historical Issues–Analysis and Decision–Making

   B. Marshal evidence of antecedent circumstances and contemporary factors contributing to problems and alternative courses of action.

   C. Identify relevant historical antecedents.

   D. Evaluate alternative courses of action.

### *Social Studies*

2. Time, Continuity and Change: Social studies programs should include experiences that provide for the study of the ways human beings view themselves in and over time.

## *Geography*

The geographically informed person knows and understands:

1. How to use maps and other geographic representations, tools, and technologies to acquire, process, and report information from a spatial perspective.
2. How to use mental maps to organize information about people, places, and environments in a spatial context.
3. How to analyze the spatial organization of people, places, and environments on earth's surface.
4. The physical and human characteristics of places.
12. The processes, patterns, and functions of human settlement.

## *Mathematics*

4. Mathematical Power
5. Problem Solving
6. Communication
8. Mathematical Concepts
9. Mathematical Procedures
10. Mathematical Disposition

### Materials Needed

**Students Need:** "Build a City!" handout with due dates filled in (see pages 117–118), pencils

**Teacher Needs:** A list of group assignments (optional)

### Steps

1. Distribute project overviews. Ask students to put their names on them immediately.
2. Place students in groups of four or fewer.
3. Go through the handout, explaining each item:

*Cause and effect essay*: This work will be based on an important decision the student made up until this point in the school year. The essay follows the usual format. You may need to review essay-writing steps (see **Chapter 1**).

*One article for your city's newspaper*: Go through some of the ideas in the "Group Responsibilities" section. Let students know that they will have a chance to look at local newspaper articles for ideas.

*One "Novel Closure" sheet* (see **Chapter 1**): Inform students that they will need to choose an appropriate book.

*A colony newspaper*: Students can choose whether they want to create a tabloid or broadsheet format.

*A biography of a famous resident of your city*: Explain that there will be a lesson around how to write a biography, using the essay format.

*A scale map of your city*: Before the model is built, students will have to work together to create a map.

*A model of the city*: Let the students know that they will receive lots of information on this and not to start building until you give them permission.

4.  Give students about 15 minutes to begin to make plans in their groups. Their goals should be to:
    Get every teammate's name written on the handout;
    Start to brainstorm ideas for their city's name;
    Begin to come up with some ideas about how their city will look, where it will be, and so forth;
    Take notes on what is discussed for future reference.

5.  Call the class back together for a brief question and answer session.

### Extensions and Modifications

How you group your students will have a major impact on the way in which each group works. If you want to give your advanced students a chance to really run with this, then create a couple of groups of students with higher abilities. Often excluding these students from the other groups you form often forces other, normally reticent, students to take leadership roles. Certainly, creating groups in where students who "get it" can work closely with those who don't also has its advantages. Depending on how your classroom works, you may even wish to allow students to create their own groups.

Name: _____ Date: _____

Teammates: _____

# Build a City! School Tools Update and Review

**Instructions:** This sheet outlines your responsibilities while creating your city. Keep this handout where you'll be able to find it and use it!

## Individual Responsibilities:

**One complete cause and effect essay about a decision you made last semester:**

    A. Pick a decision that had serious causes and serious effects.

    B. Make sure your essay has a complete thesis statement and topic paragraph.

    C. Your three body paragraphs should be in this order:

        1. Description of the decision

        2. Causes for making that decision

        3. Effects of that decision.

    D. Don't forget a concluding paragraph!

        Rough Draft Due: _____

        Final Draft Due: _____

**One article for your city's newspaper:**

    A. With your group members, choose among news stories, features, and editorials. Look at the "Group Responsibilities" section for ideas.

    B. You'll write this article on your own, with information your group creates.

        Rough Draft Due: _____

**One "Novel Closure" sheet for the book of your choice.**

        Due _____

**Active participation in all aspects of group work and discussion.**

**Completion of all homework.**

# Build a City! School Tools Update and Review
## continued

## Group Responsibilities:
A colony newspaper with:

**A biography** of a famous resident of your city:
   A. Create the life of this person as a group.
   B. Each group member writes a body paragraph: vital statistics, early life, adulthood, accomplishments.
   C. As a group, you'll divide up the responsibilities for writing the topic and concluding paragraphs.

**At least four** articles, at least one news story, one feature, and one editorial. For example: A news story on a social issue in the city, an editorial about how the government is dealing with the social issue, a feature story on what residents do for fun, a feature article about the technology used in your city, any other articles, approved in advance, you can think of.
   Rough Draft Due: _____
   Final Draft Due: _____

**One city,** consisting of:
   A. A scale map of your city
      1. Every group member must draw one–quarter of the map.
      2. A map scale must be included!
   B. A model of your city (more information on this later)
   Due: _____

# Lesson 3: Cities in the Paper

**Purpose:** To remind students of the use of the newspaper.

**Process:** Students find articles related to their own town in the newspaper.

**Payoff:** While reading about their locality, students begin to understand more about what makes a city work.

## Standards Addressed

### English Language Arts

1. Students read a wide range of print and nonprint texts to build an understanding of texts, of themselves, and of the cultures of the United States and the world; to acquire new information; to respond to the needs and demands of society and the workplace; and for personal fulfillment. Among these texts are fiction and nonfiction, classic and contemporary works.

3. Students apply a wide range of strategies to comprehend, interpret, evaluate, and appreciate texts.

5. Students apply knowledge of language structure, language conventions (e.g., spelling and punctuation), media techniques, figurative language, and genre to create, critique, and discuss print and nonprint texts.

### Social Studies

10. Civic Ideals and Practices: Social studies programs should include experiences that provide for the study of the ideals, principles, and practices of citizenship in a democratic republic.

### Geography

The geographically informed person knows and understands:

12. The processes, patterns, and functions of human settlement

## Materials Needed

**Students Need:** Newspapers, pencils, paper

## Steps

1. Inform students that they will be investigating what the newspaper has to say about the city in which they live.

2. Distribute newspapers to students. Ask them to work in pairs to find an article that talks about their city; read the article; make notes of who, what, where, when, why, and how; and as list some causes and effects from the article.

3. When students have finished, debrief the activity, having pairs present the information they found to the rest of the class. Relate the articles to the butcher paper chart of what the students know about their city.

## Extensions and Modifications

You may wish to give students these three options: work alone, work with a partner, or work with you. Invite students who will have difficulty with this assignment to sit with your group. Have the students in your group "help" choose an article to read. Then, either read it while the group follows along or have volunteers in the group read a paragraph at a time. Next, while each student writes on his or her own piece of paper, facilitate a discussion of the answers to the assignment.

# Lesson 4: The Biography

**Purpose:** To introduce another essay format for students to use.

**Process:** Students watch as the teacher outlines a biographical essay.

**Payoff:** Students begin to organize the many details of a person's life into a cogent work.

## Standards Addressed

### English Language Arts

4. Students adjust their use of spoken, written, and visual language (e.g., conventions, style, vocabulary) to communicate effectively with a variety of audiences for a variety of purposes.

5. Students apply knowledge of language structure, language conventions (e.g., spelling and punctuation), media techniques, figurative language, and genre to create, critique, and discuss print and nonprint texts.

12. Students use spoken, written, and visual language to accomplish their own purposes (e.g., for learning, enjoyment, persuasion, and the exchange of information).

### Social Studies

5. Individuals, Groups and Institutions: Social studies programs should include experiences that provide for the study of interactions among individuals, groups, and institutions.

## Materials Needed

**Students Need:** Pencils, paper

**Teacher Needs:** Overhead projector, blank transparencies, "Biographical Data of Lucy Lawless" (see page 123), transparency markers

## Steps

1. Have students help you review essay format, while you make notes on a blank transparency. Remind them of the basic structure, then explain that this format can be changed slightly for writing a biography.

2. Ask students what kinds of information are usually included in a biography. Make a list of their ideas.

3. Ask students to help you group their ideas into these four categories:

*Vital Statistics:* The basics, like dates of birth and death, where the person was born and lived, other important relationships (famous relatives, spouse, children).

*Early Life:* Important childhood events that influenced the later actions that made this person famous. Advanced students may see some of these events as "causes" in a chain.

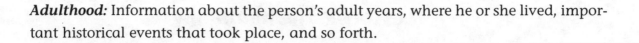
*Adulthood:* Information about the person's adult years, where he or she lived, important historical events that took place, and so forth.

*Accomplishments:* The reasons that this person is noteworthy and the effects of this person on others.

4. Write down the biographical information of Lucy Lawless. (If desired, you can copy this information onto a transparency in advance.) Have students help you categorize each line. Decide if any information is interesting but not important enough to include in the biography.

5. Explain that a biographical essay comprises six paragraphs, instead of the usual five. Ask students how many body paragraphs will be in such an essay (four). Ask students how many sentences will make up the topic paragraph (five: the thesis statement, plus the four rewritten topic sentences from the body paragraphs).

6. Explain to students that one way to organize the many pieces of information involved in a biography is to place each piece into the four categories you have shown them. Tell the students that for their fictional biography (of an important resident of the cities they are creating) they need to use these categories.

7. Using the information provided, create an outline of the body paragraphs for a biography of Lucy Lawless.

8. Explain how to write the final work, modeling how to write the topic paragraph the usual way (thesis statement, rewritten topic sentences in reverse order).

9. Give students time to begin creating data around their fictional city resident.

## Extensions and Modifications

Some students may need to collect biographical information, put it into chronological order, then separate it into four logical parts (childhood, early adulthood, adulthood, summary of accomplishments). A four-column chart, with those headings, on which a student could write each point would also be helpful.

# Biographical Data of Lucy Lawless
### (the actress who plays *Xena: Warrior Princess*)

- Born in 1968

- Her name was Lucy Ryan

- Has four brothers and one sister

- Grew up in New Zealand

- Described as a "tomboy" during childhood

- Performed in school plays and musicals

- Went to private schools

- First job was as a gold miner in a camp in the Australian outback

- Married Garth Lawless

- Moved back to New Zealand to have a baby

- Daughter's name is Daisy

- At age 20, appeared in a comedy show called "Funny Business"

- Mrs. New Zealand, 1989

- Studied acting in Canada in 1992

- Her teacher was Bill Davis, who now plays the "Smoking Man" on the show *X-Files*

- Became the co-host of a travel show called *Air New Zealand Holiday*

- Played roles in TV shows and movies, including *The New Adventures of the Black Stallion*

- In 1994, she played Lysia, the Amazon on the first *Hercules* show

- In 1995, she played Lyla in two other *Hercules* episodes

- Played Xena in three *Hercules* episodes before her series was created

- *Xena: Warrior Princess*, with a strong woman hero, became popular in many countries

# Lesson 5: More on Editing

**Purpose:** To introduce an editing tool for students to use with their peers.

**Process:** Using an example of writing from a brave student, the class completes peer editing sheets with the teacher's facilitation.

**Payoff:** Students begin to be able to edit each other's work.

## Standards Addressed

### *English Language Arts*

5. Students apply knowledge of language structure, language conventions (e.g., spelling and punctuation), media techniques, figurative language, and genre to create, critique, and discuss print and nonprint texts.

## Materials Needed

**Students Need:** "Peer Editing Checklist" sheet (see page 126), pencils

**Teacher Needs:** A transparency of an example of student work (feel free to copy one of the examples in **Chapter 1**), a transparency of the "Peer Editing Checklist" (see page 126), transparency markers, overhead projector, blank transparencies (just in case)

## Steps

1. Explain that a brave student is taking a risk by allowing the class to see his or her work and to edit it. Set some expectations of behavior.

2. Go over the "Peer Editing Checklist" explaining that it is a useful tool to use when students are reading each others' work. (You may wish to make it a mandatory part of editing.) Have students participate in explaining why different elements of the sheet are important in writing. Define "Easy Words" for your grade level. (We often called them "No Excuse Words.") These are simple, basic words that students should not be misspelling at their current grade level.

3. On the transparency, fill out the Author, Editor, Date, and Title spaces.

4. Show the transparency of the student work. To edit this as a class, read each sentence out loud and have students raise their hands if there are errors to correct. Have them assist you in replacing them (occasionally, you will be the only one to see them).

5. Once you have covered the entire piece of work, go through the "Peer Editing Checklist" and check off the appropriate boxes, referring back to the written work. Have students do the same task on their own sheets.

6. Ask students for some "glows and grows," or things they liked about the writing and things they would suggest changing. Have each student write down one of each type

of comment on his or her "Peer Editing Checklist." Write one of each on your transparency of the checklist.

7. Encourage students to use these checklists when editing each others' city work.

## Extensions and Modifications

You may need to be the peer editor a few times for some of your students. Another option is to sit with pairs of students while they edit each other's work and coach them along. If you have a group of students who show exceptional promise, you may wish to create a cadre of editors. These students, when caught up in their own assignments, could be in charge of editing and revising other students' work.

## Peer Editing Checklist

Author: _____

Editor: _____

Date: _____

Title: _____

Punctuation:
- ☐ Periods
- ☐ Capitals

Spelling:
- ☐ Easy Words
- ☐ Other Words

Paragraphs:
- ☐ There's an Outline
- ☐ Indent
- ☐ Topic Sentence

Writing:
- ☐ Follows Outline
- ☐ Makes Sense
- ☐ Interesting Words

Comments:

## Peer Editing Checklist

Author: _____

Editor: _____

Date: _____

Title: _____

Punctuation:
- ☐ Periods
- ☐ Capitals

Spelling:
- ☐ Easy Words
- ☐ Other Words

Paragraphs:
- ☐ There's an Outline
- ☐ Indent
- ☐ Topic Sentence

Writing:
- ☐ Follows Outline
- ☐ Makes Sense
- ☐ Interesting Words

Comments:

## Peer Editing Checklist

Author: _____

Editor: _____

Date: _____

Title: _____

Punctuation:
- ☐ Periods
- ☐ Capitals

Spelling:
- ☐ Easy Words
- ☐ Other Words

Paragraphs:
- ☐ There's an Outline
- ☐ Indent
- ☐ Topic Sentence

Writing:
- ☐ Follows Outline
- ☐ Makes Sense
- ☐ Interesting Words

Comments:

# Lesson 6: Creating a Map

**Purpose:** Students review the function and components of maps.

**Process:** After a brief lesson, students work individually to create maps of their cities.

**Payoff:** Students have maps from which to build their city models.

## Standards Addressed

### *Geography*

The geographically informed person knows and understands:

1. How to use maps and other geographic representations, tools, and technologies to acquire, process, and report information from a spatial perspective.

2. How to use mental maps to organize information about people, places, and environments in a spatial context.

3. How to analyze the spatial organization of people, places, and environments on earth's surface.

4. The physical and human characteristics of places.

12. The processes, patterns, and functions of human settlement.

### *Mathematics*

4. Mathematical Power
6. Communication
8. Mathematical Concepts
9. Mathematical Procedures
10. Mathematical Disposition

## Materials Needed

**Students Need:** Pencils, graph paper

**Teacher Needs:** Butcher paper, markers

## Steps

1. Title the butcher paper "City Maps." Next, as a subtitle, write, "What belongs on a map" and have students brainstorm map components (compass rose, scale, streets, rivers, and so forth). Put a star next to the components that you will require on every map.

2. Write a second subtitle, "What belongs in a city" and have students brainstorm different things that might appear on a city map (points of interest, important buildings, and so forth).

3. Inform students that before they will be able to create models of their cities, they will need to create a map. First, though, they will work individually to create maps of their cities, which they will use when planning as a group.

4. Pass out the graph paper and ask students to put their names and the names of their cities on the back.

5. Ask the students to look at the grid blocks and make scale recommendations. Help them to discover what units each line segment (or side of a square) should equal. Should the scale be one segment equals one foot? Ten feet? A meter? You may want to tape a piece of paper up where everyone can see, where you can model how a street might look, given a certain scale. Also, remind students that they must have the essential components on their maps. Show them how the scale might be drawn.

6. Give students plenty of time to work with their maps. They may need several sheets of grid paper before they get what they like. Remind the students that later they will work in their groups to combine ideas.

## Extensions and Modifications

Some students will really need your help in creating scale drawings of their city ideas. You may recommend that they create their cities using the grid lines as streets, to keep things a little more simple. It is easier to plan a city without winding roads.

# Lesson 7: City Planning

**Purpose:** Students use each other as resources to review map skills.

**Process:** Students work on teams to develop a central theme and a unified city map.

**Payoff:** When they have completed their maps, groups will be ready to build their cities.

## Standards Addressed

### *Geography*

The geographically informed person knows and understands:

1. How to use maps and other geographic representations, tools, and technologies to acquire, process, and report information from a spatial perspective.

2. How to use mental maps to organize information about people, places, and environments in a spatial context.

3. How to analyze the spatial organization of people, places, and environments on earth's surface.

4. The physical and human characteristics of places.

12. The processes, patterns, and functions of human settlement.

### *Mathematics*

4. Mathematical Power

6. Communication

8. Mathematical Concepts

9. Mathematical Procedures

10. Mathematical Disposition

## Materials Needed

**Students Need:** Graph paper, notebook paper, pencils, completed maps from Lesson 6

## Steps

1. Inform students that today they will start work on creating group maps for their cities. Explain that they have two tasks to complete before drafting the map. The first is to decide on a theme for their city (for example, out in space, underground, a landlocked city, a coastal city, a mountain town). Ask them to brainstorm themes on notebook paper, then decide as a group which one they prefer. The second step is to share individual maps, check the scale, then talk about which ideas from each person's map should be integrated into the group map. These ideas should also be listed on a piece of paper. Tell students that they must show you these two sets of completed notes before beginning the next step.

2. When student groups come to you for approval, gauge student buy-in, checking to make sure each group member feels included in the decision-making process. If disagreements exist, or if either set of notes is not detailed to your expectations, send the group back to try again.

3. When a group has completed the notes, allow the students within the group to work together on a unified map. Remind groups to include the essential components outlined in Lesson 6.

4. Completion of maps may take two or three 20-minute work sessions.

## Extensions and Modifications

Some groups may need extra encouragement in creating either more simplified or more complicated maps, depending on their collective focus and aptitudes.

# Lesson 8: Creating a Tribune

**Purpose:** To give students a framework from which to build their newspapers.

**Process:** Students look at the local paper for structures and ideas.

**Payoff:** Students are able to develop a plan for creating their city newspapers.

## Standards Addressed

### *English Language Arts*

4. Students adjust their use of spoken, written, and visual language (e.g., conventions, style, vocabulary) to communicate effectively with a variety of audiences for a variety of purposes.

5. Students apply knowledge of language structure, language conventions (e.g., spelling and punctuation), media techniques, figurative language, and genre to create, critique, and discuss print and nonprint texts.

12. Students use spoken, written, and visual language to accomplish their own purposes (e.g., for learning, enjoyment, persuasion, and the exchange of information).

### *National Center for History in the Schools: Historical Thinking*

Standard 1. Chronological Thinking

A. Distinguish between past, present, and future time.

B. Identify in historical narratives the temporal structure of a historical narrative or story.

C. Establish temporal order in constructing historical narratives of their own.

## Materials Needed

**Students Need:** A newspaper for each city group

**Teacher Needs:** A newspaper

## Steps

1. Inform the students that they will be looking through their newspapers to get ideas for the way in which they will design their city papers.

2. Pass out a newspaper to each group. Instruct the students to divide up sections of the newspaper within their groups and discuss aspects of the paper they would like to include in their own newspapers.

3. Walk around the room, facilitating discussion. Draw students' attention to where advertisements are located, how the weather is depicted, table of contents, and so forth.

4. When discussions begin to lag, remind students that each member of the group needs to write an article about the city. You may wish to have them look back over their handouts.

5. Give students time to begin writing rough drafts of their articles.

6. Be sure to provide independent work time during the week and reserve some time for groups to work on putting their newspapers together.

## Extensions and Modifications

Depending on how you have grouped your students, some city teams may need extra time to work together. Another option is to create priority checklists for individuals during unstructured work time ("first, you need to finish this, then this"), so students have some help in managing their time. Other groups may wish to get very creative with their newspapers and should be encouraged to write extra articles and add features (horoscopes, TV listings, comics, and so forth).

# Lesson 9: Creating a City

**Purpose:** To get students into the actual construction of their models.

**Process:** The teacher informs students of the building process.

**Payoff:** Students get to put together really exciting models.

## Standards Addressed

### *Geography*

The geographically informed person knows and understands:

1. How to use maps and other geographic representations, tools, and technologies to acquire, process, and report information from a spatial perspective.
2. How to use mental maps to organize information about people, places, and environments in a spatial context.
3. How to analyze the spatial organization of people, places, and environments on earth's surface.
4. The physical and human characteristics of places.
12. The processes, patterns, and functions of human settlement.

### *Mathematics*

4. Mathematical Power
6. Communication
8. Mathematical Concepts
9. Mathematical Procedures
10. Mathematical Disposition

## Materials Needed

**Students Need:** City maps, notebook paper, pencils

**Teacher Needs:** A place to write student brainstorms

## Steps

1. Let students know that they will begin to create their city models as soon as their scale maps are completed correctly.
2. Tell students that their city models cannot be any larger than four square feet. You may wish to draw an approximation of this size on the board (two feet by two feet). Explain that students may use any materials that they either bring from home or that you provide. Write down the kinds of things you are willing to provide (for example, construction paper, tape).
3. Ask students to brainstorm the kinds of supplies they might contribute, that would help make their city model interesting. Write their brainstorms on the board.

4. Inform students that once you have approved their final city maps, they will need to provide you with a detailed supplies list, with a star next to the materials they need you to contribute.

5. Give students time to work. When teams bring their city map for you to inspect, do a necessary elements "spot-check," where you make sure the map is completed to your expectations.

6. Require the supplies list to be specific, even listing how many pieces of construction paper, and of which colors, they will need. In the long run, this will make your job easier, because you can compile all of these materials at once.

7. Provide model building time, perhaps three half-hour sessions, or if your students can handle it, provide longer work sessions, where they can choose to complete any aspect of the unit (writing, reading, creating newspapers, maps, and so forth).

## Extensions and modifications

Some student groups may need the extra challenge of creating a budget for their cities. This could entail finding out materials costs (by calling for example, construction companies, hardware stores), land values, and so forth. In fact, this entire aspect of the unit can be expanded into a problem-solving exercise, complete with reports, specifically scaled models, and the like.

# Lesson 10: City Presentations

**Purpose:** To give students a chance to share their creative endeavors.

**Process:** Student groups share their models and newspaper.

**Payoff:** The class gets to see the fruits of its labor.

## Standards Addressed

### *Geography*

The geographically informed person knows and understands:

   12. The processes, patterns, and functions of human settlement.

## Materials Needed

**Students need:** Completed "City Information" slips (see page 136)

## Steps

1. A few days before the due date, tell the students when they will be presenting their completed models. Explain that groups will share their newspapers and the design and concepts of their cities, then leave their cities and newspapers on display for a few days.

2. On the day of the presentations, have students gather in a spot where they can see each city as it is presented.

3. Call groups one by one to describe their cities, point out areas of interest, explain how they constructed them, and so forth. Allow students a few minutes to share their newspapers. Give other students a chance to ask questions of the presenting group.

4. Have students fill out the information slips, to post next to their projects.

5. Leave the cities and their newspapers in a safe spot, where students can explore other groups' work.

## Extensions and Modifications

Not all students will be comfortable taking part in the presentations. You may either require every group member to have a speaking part or let some students off the hook by allowing them to be pointers and sign holders. If some groups have really taken off, you may suggest they turn their presentations into "infomercials" in which they try to persuade others to move to their cities (a video or other visual aids would also be appropriate).

## Cities Information

Name: _____

Date: _____

Name of City:

Location of City:

City Designers:

Cool Info:

## Cities Information

Name: _____

Date: _____

Name of City:

Location of City:

City Designers:

Cool Info:

## Chapter 7
# End of Year Review Unit:
### School Tools Redux

## Introduction

In this week-long culmination, students use the School Tools one more time under your supervision. They pick and choose from several lists of possible assignments to prove their proficiency with each tool. This unit allows you to assess each student's abilities, but also provides a final reminder of the tools' utility to your students.

For writing, students will be required to complete one of the writing forms learned over the school year. Thus, they can choose to write an essay, a short story, a persuasive essay, or a biography.

Individually, in pairs, and as a large group, students will complete several cause and effect analyses to drive home the importance of looking for the causes and effects in their lives. They will be given the choice of analyzing a current event that occurred during the course of the school year or a book they have read in the last few months. In pairs, they will make cause and effect predictions for the coming school year. As a whole group, they will create a cause and effect chart of your behavior, for the reference of future students!

Students will finalize math facts scores and analyze their progress. They will complete one more problem-solving report, and each student will create a scale map of the school (or classroom) for next year's students.

Obviously, if these assignments are too concentrated and intense for the last weeks of school, feel free to choose the lessons that will best allow you to track and evaluate your students' use of the School Tools.

# Lesson 1: The Final Chapter:
# A Backwards Glance at the Future

**Purpose:** To provide students with an overview of their assignments.

**Process:** The teacher passes out the assignment list and explains its components.

**Payoff:** Students can begin to work independently.

## Standards Addressed

### *English Language Arts*

4. Students adjust their use of spoken, written, and visual language (e.g., conventions, style, vocabulary) to communicate effectively with a variety of audiences for a variety of purposes.

5. Students apply knowledge of language structure, language conventions (e.g., spelling and punctuation), media techniques, figurative language, and genre to create, critique, and discuss print and nonprint texts.

12. Students use spoken, written, and visual language to accomplish their own purposes (e.g., for learning, enjoyment, persuasion, and the exchange of information).

### *National Center for History in the Schools: Historical Thinking*

Standard 1. Chronological Thinking

A. Distinguish between past, present, and future time.

B. Identify in historical narratives the temporal structure of a historical narrative or story.

C. Establish temporal order in constructing historical narratives of their own.

Standard 3. Historical Analysis and Interpretation

E. Analyze cause-and-effect relationships and multiple causation, including the importance of the individual, the influence of ideas, and the role of chance.

J. Hypothesize the influence of the past.

Standard 5. Historical Issues–Analysis and Decision–Making

B. Marshal evidence of antecedent circumstances and contemporary factors contributing to problems and alternative courses of action.

C. Identify relevant historical antecedents.

D. Evaluate alternative courses of action.

### *Social Studies*

2. Time, Continuity and Change: Social studies programs should include experiences that provide for the study of the ways human beings view themselves in and over time.

*Geography*

The geographically informed person knows and understands:

1. How to use maps and other geographic representations, tools, and technologies to acquire, process, and report information from a spatial perspective.
2. How to use mental maps to organize information about people, places, and environments in a spatial context.
3. How to analyze the spatial organization of people, places, and environments on earth's surface.
4. The physical and human characteristics of places.

*Mathematics*

4. Mathematical Power
5. Problem Solving
6. Communication
8. Mathematical Concepts
9. Mathematical Procedures
10. Mathematical Disposition

## Materials Needed

**Students Need:** "School Tools Redux" (see page 140–141), pencils

**Teacher Needs:** "School Tools Redux" (see page 140–141)

## Steps

1. Explain to students that they will be given the chance to demonstrate how well they can use the School Tools. Remind them that these tools will be useful in the following school years, so this is also a chance to review them one more time.
2. Pass out "School Tools Redux" and explain each section. Set deadlines as appropriate. For the writing assignments, you may wish to make handouts from **Chapters 1** and **7** available. Inform students that the scale-map assignment will have more explanation in the near future.
3. Give the students time to begin planning their assignments.

## Extensions and Modifications

You may wish to scale back some of the assignments for students who are overwhelmed. On the other hand, some students may be capable of doing more work, such as completing two writing assignments.

# School Tools Redux: A Backward Glance to the Future

**Instructions:** Your responsibilities during this mini-unit will be as follows:

### On Your Own:

### Complete at least one of the following:

An essay

A short story

A persuasive essay

A biography

*You must follow the proper format, and provide the following:*

An outline

A rough draft

A final draft

Due: _____

### Do a cause and effect analysis of one of the following:

A current event that occurred during the school year

An important decision you made this school year

Please provide the following:

A paragraph describing the event

A cause and effect T–chart for the event

Due: _____

# School Tools Redux: A Backward Glance to the Future
## continued

**Create one math problem-solving report**

Consider an important math problem in your life and write a complete report on how it could be solved. Use the "Problem Solving Report" format.

Be sure to include:

    A rough draft

    A final draft

Due: _____

**Draw a scale map of the school for use by a new student**

Don't forget:

    A scale, labels

Due: _____

**With a Friend:**

**Develop a cause and effect analysis chart with predictions for next year!**

    Be sure to include causes from this school year that will lead to effects next year.

Due: _____

You will also be expected to complete homework and other work, as assigned.

# Lesson 2: Review of Cause and Effect Analysis

**Purpose:** To remind students how to complete a cause and effect analysis.

**Process:** The class analyzes a short article from the newspaper.

**Payoff:** Students are ready to begin this aspect of their assignments.

## Standards Addressed

### National Center for History in the Schools: Historical Thinking

Standard 1. Chronological Thinking

    A. Distinguish between past, present, and future time.

    B. Identify in historical narratives the temporal structure of a historical narrative or story.

    C. Establish temporal order in constructing historical narratives of their own.

Standard 3. Historical Analysis and Interpretation

    E. Analyze cause-and-effect relationships and multiple causation, including the importance of the individual, the influence of ideas, and the role of chance.

    J. Hypothesize the influence of the past.

Standard 5. Historical Issues-Analysis and Decision-Making

    B. Marshal evidence of antecedent circumstances and contemporary factors contributing to problems and alternative courses of action.

    C. Identify relevant historical antecedents.

    D. Evaluate alternative courses of action.

### Social Studies

    2. Time, Continuity and Change: Social studies programs should include experiences that provide for the study of the ways human beings view themselves in and over time.

## Materials Needed

**Teacher Needs:** A newspaper, one transparency copy of the article to be used, two blank transparencies, overhead markers, overhead projector

## Steps

1. In a large group forum, ask students to explain how and why it is useful to find cause and effect relationships in reading, history, personal life, and so forth.

2. Remind students that they will be completing such an analysis as part of their "School Tools Redux" assignments. Tell them that as a class you will complete an analysis on a short newspaper article.

3. Put the article transparency on the projector and read it to the class (or have students assist in reading it aloud).

4. Ask students to paraphrase the pertinent details of the article. On a blank sheet, take notes. You may want to remind students to use "who, what, where, when, why, and how" to structure a response. Remind them that an overview is an important part of their analysis.

5. Draw a cause and effect T–chart on the second sheet. Ask students to volunteer cause and effect relationships they noticed. Encourage them to use only the article's information at first, then allow the students to identify relationships based on what they may know from other sources. Finally ask students to make logical predictions from the article, about future cause and effect relationships. Explain to students that they should fully analyze the information within the text of the article before going beyond it.

6. Give students some time to begin creating their own analyses based on the assignments in the "School Tools Redux" handout (see page 140–141).

## Extensions and Modifications

Some students may wish to use the "Who, what, where, when, and why" handout from **Chapter 2** (page 46) as a structure when completing their own analyses. You might encourage other students to further research the events they study, to provide a more in-depth cause and effect analysis.

# Lesson 3: Looking Back: Editing Previous Work

**Purpose:** Students are given the chance to edit work from earlier in the year.

**Process:** The teacher uses a brave student's example to remind students how to revise their work.

**Payoff:** Students can see how their writing skills have improved.

## Standards Addressed

### English Language Arts

4. Students adjust their use of spoken, written, and visual language (e.g., conventions, style, vocabulary) to communicate effectively with a variety of audiences for a variety of purposes.

5. Students apply knowledge of language structure, language conventions (e.g., spelling and punctuation), media techniques, figurative language, and genre to create, critique, and discuss print and nonprint texts.

12. Students use spoken, written, and visual language to accomplish their own purposes (e.g., for learning, enjoyment, persuasion, and the exchange of information).

## Materials Needed

**Students Need:** Paper, pencils, old writing assignments

**Teacher Needs:** A transparency of an example of student work (feel free to copy one of the examples in **Chapter 1**), one transparency of the "Peer Editing Checklist" (see page 126), transparency markers, overhead projector, blank transparencies (just in case)

## Steps

1. Explain that a brave student is taking a risk by allowing the class to see his or her work and to edit it. Remind students of respectful behavior.

2. Show the transparency of the student work. Ask students for some "glows and grows," or things they liked about the writing and things they would suggest changing. Have each student write down one of each type of comment on his or her "Peer Editing Checklist." Write one of each on your transparency of the checklist. Hopefully, editing errors will be few, so you can really concentrate on form, vocabulary, and style.

3. Give students time to edit a piece of writing. You may wish to encourage students to use "Peer Editing Checklists" (page 126) when editing their own work.

4. Circulate around the room, facilitating the process and eliciting comments about how student writing ability has changed over the school year. You may wish to ask students to write a short reflection paragraph describing these changes.

## Extensions and Modifications

Some students may work better with your direct coaching or in pairs with students they trust.

# Lesson 4: Finalize Math Facts Scores

**Purpose:** To give students a sense of accomplishment about math facts (we hope).

**Process:** Students create a line graph, documenting their math facts progress.

**Payoff:** Students have a graphic representation of their hard work.

## Standards Addressed

### *Mathematics*

4. Mathematical Power
8. Mathematical Concepts
9. Mathematical Procedures
10. Mathematical Disposition

## Materials Needed

**Students Need:** Their "Math Facts Tracking Sheets" (see page 80), graph paper, pencils

**Teacher Needs:** Graph paper transparency, overhead markers, overhead projector

## Steps

1. Ask students if they believe their ability in math facts has improved. Have students explain some of the strategies they used over the school year to become better in timed tests. Explain that today they will be creating graphs to see how their work has changed.

2. On the overhead, model how you'd create a math facts line graph. Explain that students will create a graph for each operation (that is, one for multiplication, one for addition, and so forth). If you have been taking the tests, use your own data. Otherwise, make some up. Show students how to write the dates of each test along the bottom, long edge of the paper. Depending on the way in which you scored the tests, you may need to set appropriate intervals for the Y–axis, where scores will be figured. Label the X–axis "Date" and the Y–axis "Score" or "Time." Create the line graph, connecting points.

3. Give students time to use their own data to create graphs. Circulate around the classroom, assisting students and noting their results.

## Extensions and Modifications

Some students may not show much or any progress. You may wish to encourage these students by finding other areas in which they did well. (You will know best how to deal with your students.)

# Lesson 5: Problem–Solving Report

**Purpose:**  To review the "Mathematical Problem Format."
**Process:**  The class goes over the handout and brainstorms ideas.
**Payoff:**  Students are ready to begin their reports.

## Standards Addressed

### English Language Arts

3. Students apply a wide range of strategies to comprehend, interpret, evaluate, and appreciate texts.
4. Students adjust their use of spoken, written, and visual language (e.g., conventions, style, vocabulary) to communicate effectively with a variety of audiences for a variety of purposes.

### Mathematics

4. Mathematical Power
5. Problem Solving
6. Communication
8. Mathematical Concepts
9. Mathematical Procedures
10. Mathematical Disposition

## Materials Needed

**Students Need:**  "Mathematics Problem Format" handout (see page 147)
**Teacher Needs:**  "Mathematics Problem Format" handout (see page 147)

## Steps

1. Distribute the handout to the students.
2. Brainstorm with students some possible problems to solve. I have had students try to figure out how much money would be required to repaint and recarpet their bedrooms, build a fence around their yards, or drive to Las Vegas and stay for a few days.
3. Give the students some time to get started.

## Extensions and Modifications

Some students may need prescriptive, step-by-step assistance, while others may just need some help devising a problem to solve. Encourage students to make their problems more or less complex, depending on ability. Some students' problems may involve phone calls to businesses, research into costs, and so forth.

Name:_____ Date: _____

# Mathematics Problem Format

Your mathematics problem report will be a polished project. Develop a problem to solve whose answers might be useful to you. Get your teacher's approval before beginning. Each of the following should be a separate, neatly written section of the report.

I. *The Problem:* State exactly what the problem is and what you will be including in the solution.

II. *Considerations:* What kinds of things will you need to figure out? What information will you need, and where will you get it?

III. *Calculations:* Show all of your math, labeling what each number means.

IV. *Solutions:* Refer back to what you said you would solve in The Problem. Clearly discuss all points of your solution and explain how you found your answers.

V. *Conclusion:* What did you learn? How could you simplify the problem? What is another way to solve it?

# Lesson 6: Scale Map of School for Next Year's Students

**Purpose:**  Students get a final review of map components.

**Process:**  Students work to create maps of the school.

**Payoff:**  Finished maps provide evidence of understanding.

## Standards Addressed

### *Geography*

The geographically informed person knows and understands:

1. How to use maps and other geographic representations, tools, and technologies to acquire, process, and report information from a spatial perspective.

2. How to use mental maps to organize information about people, places, and environments in a spatial context.

3. How to analyze the spatial organization of people, places, and environments on earth's surface.

4. The physical and human characteristics of places.

### *Mathematics*

4. Mathematical Power

6. Communication

8. Mathematical Concepts

9. Mathematical Procedures

10. Mathematical Disposition

## Materials Needed

**Students Need:**  Graph paper, pencils, measurement tools

## Steps

1. Have students gather, review the meaning of scale, and make a list of essential map components.

2. Ask students how a scale drawing of the school might be useful to a new student. Next, get ideas on how this map might be completed in an efficient and correct way, without disturbing other teachers or students.

3. Instruct students to work individually to make a scale drawing of the school. You may wish to send out small groups at a time to keep crowds down.

4. After students have completed the exercise, gather them to debrief. Discuss problems and solutions, brainstorms, and so forth.

6. Collect drawings to see who "gets it."

**Extensions and Modifications**

You may need to work closely with certain students or make the assignment more manageable (say, sketch a model of the shape of the classroom only, roughly to scale, or just measure the walls in the building). You may also wish to work with a small group of students who need extra attention and help. Some students will be able to add a great deal of detail to their maps.

# Lesson 7: Cause and Effect Predictions

**Purpose:**  Students use their knowledge about cause and effect to make predictions.

**Process:**  The class "warms up" with a few attempts.

**Payoff:**  Students begin to think about their ability to influence cause and effect relationships to their own benefit.

## Standards Addressed
### *National Center for History in the Schools: Historical Thinking*

Standard 1. Chronological Thinking

  A.  Distinguish between past, present, and future time.

  B.  Identify in historical narratives the temporal structure of a historical narrative or story.

  C.  Establish temporal order in constructing historical narratives of their own.

Standard 3. Historical Analysis and Interpretation

  E.  Analyze cause-and-effect relationships and multiple causation, including the importance of the individual, the influence of ideas, and the role of chance.

  J.  Hypothesize the influence of the past.

Standard 5. Historical Issues–Analysis and Decision–Making

  B.  Marshal evidence of antecedent circumstances and contemporary factors contributing to problems and alternative courses of action.

  C.  Identify relevant historical antecedents.

  D.  Evaluate alternative courses of action.

### *Social Studies*

  2.  Time, Continuity and Change: Social studies programs should include experiences that provide for the study of the ways human beings view themselves in and over time.

## Materials Needed

**Students Need:** Paper, pencils

## Steps

1. Ask students to volunteer things that happened during this school year that will influence the following year. Have someone explain why those events are possible "causes" for next year's effects.

2. Explain to students that, as part of their School Tools assignments, they need to work in pairs to make predictions of effects, based on causes from this school year. Remind the students how to create T–charts.

3. Give the students plenty of time to work on these.

4. Debrief by discussing with your students how they could have an influence on what effects come from this school year. Concentrate on encouraging your students to take responsibility for their roles in cause and effect relationships.

# Lesson 8: Fair Warning for Future Students

**Purpose:** To give the students a fun way to use causal relationships.

**Process:** Students brainstorm the cause and effect relationships that exist in the teacher's classroom.

**Payoff:** Students and the teacher get some closure around the end of the year.

## Standards Addressed

### *National Center for History in the Schools: Historical Thinking*

Standard 1. Chronological Thinking

    A. Distinguish between past, present, and future time.

    B. Identify in historical narratives the temporal structure of a historical narrative or story.

    C. Establish temporal order in constructing historical narratives of their own.

Standard 3. Historical Analysis and Interpretation

    E. Analyze cause-and-effect relationships and multiple causation, including the importance of the individual, the influence of ideas, and the role of chance.

    J. Hypothesize the influence of the past.

Standard 5. Historical Issues–Analysis and Decision–Making

    B. Marshal evidence of antecedent circumstances and contemporary factors contributing to problems and alternative courses of action.

    C. Identify relevant historical antecedents.

    D. Evaluate alternative courses of action.

### *Social Studies*

    2. Time, Continuity and Change: Social studies programs should include experiences that provide for the study of the ways human beings view themselves in and over time.

## Materials Needed

**Students Need:** Paper, pencils

**Teacher Needs:** Patience, a sense of humor

## Steps

1. In a large group setting, ask students why recognizing cause and effect relationships can be a useful tool when encountering a new situation.

2. Explain that the students will be creating T–charts of cause and effect relationships that exist in your (the teacher's) classroom, which you will read to next year's students at the beginning of the school year.

3. Ask for some examples of these relationships, to get the students started.

4. Tell the students that they will have the chance to read their charts, if they so desire, once everyone has finished.

5. Give the students time to work, then laugh and laugh when they read their charts to the class.

6. Save the charts to kick off next year's School Tools unit!

# Glossary

**Analysis:** In an experiment or observation, the analysis explains what occurred, what was learned, and what could be done differently next time.

**Application:** The fourth step in the School Tools learning process where a tool is used by a student in a content area.

**Biographical essay:** Nonfiction, six-paragraph essay, in which the first three body paragraphs divide personal data into categories (for example, early life, accomplishments, vital statistics) and the fourth is an analysis or synthesis.

**Broadsheet:** The format of a newspaper that opens into large, contiguous sheets. Opposite of a tabloid, which opens like a book.

**Cause and effect analysis:** Where issues are placed on a T–chart, then causes and effects are generated around them.

**Cause and effect relationships:** Chains of events where the stimuli and reactions are either known, predicted, or theoretical.

**Century Books:** A project, using cause and effect in social studies. For every conflict studied, students created at least one page on political, economic, and social causes; one page on political, economic, and social effects; and one creative page.

**Chronology:** A time-ordered list of events.

**Conclusion:** Answers the question, "Did the experiment prove the hypothesis to be valid?"

**Economic:** Relating to finance, money, or trade.

**Editorial:** Expresses the opinions of the writer. It is usually placed in a specific section of a newspaper to set it apart from factual stories. Some editorials express the opinions of the publishers, while others can be written by columnists or readers.

**Emotional:** Describes human feelings.

**Essay:** A form of nonfiction writing, which is written in a concise format.

**Events:** Discrete occurrences in simple stories.

**Exercise:** The third phase in the School Tools learning process where a tool is used in a very prescriptive and supervised way.

**Experiment:** Performance of certain tasks to prove a hypothesis.

**Expository writing:** Nonfiction writing with a purpose.

**Feature article:** Tends to be about people's personal lives, fashion, culture, or entertainment. Can be lighthearted or serious. It has plenty of facts, but the opinion of the author may be evident.

**Guided Practice:** The second phase in the School Tools learning process where the student goes through a step-by-step learning process with teacher supervision.

**Hypothesis:** An educated guess about what will occur in a given experiment.

**Introduction:** The first phase in the School Tools learning process that is a student's first exposure to a new School Tool.

**Math facts:** Basic algorithms of computation in addition, subtraction, multiplication, and division. Most math facts use numbers 1 through 12.

**Mini-essay:** A short, expository piece, with a thesis statement, three body paragraphs, and a concluding statement.

**News story:** Written in an objective way, it provides factual information about events without expressing the writer's opinion.

**Novel closure:** A final effort by the student on completing the reading of a novel. Its purpose is to give the student a chance to make connections and conclusions in his or her reading and to demonstrate understanding of what was read.

**NPR:** National Public Radio. Like Public Broadcasting Service, but on the air. Provides in-depth news coverage that can prove useful when making up homework assignments.

**Observation:** Students watching while the teacher performs a science activity. No hypothesis is made beforehand.

**Persuasive essays:** Written works with the purpose of convincing someone of one's position.

**Physical:** Relating to concrete, observable occurrences.

**Political:** Relating to government.

**Quick writes:** Short, 10- to 15-minute assignments, which force students to practice extemporaneous writing for a purpose.

**Reliability:** When an experiment can be repeated with the same results every time.

**Risk:** The final School Tools learning stage, at which point the student is able to use a tool and modify it to his or her needs.

**School Tools:** Essential skills students need to be successful. These are basic formats or cognitive organizers, that allow students to categorize information as it arrives.

**Setting:** Where and when a story takes place.

**Simple story format:** A five-paragraph story. The first paragraph introduces the setting, characters, and problem. The three subsequent paragraphs each describe an event in the story. Conclusion of the plot is the purpose of the fifth paragraph.

**Social:** Relating to groups of people.

**T–chart:** A two-column chart, used for comparison or to align ideas. Often used for cause and effect or compare–contrast activities.

**Tabloid:** A newspaper format in which the pages open like a book. Opposite of a broadsheet.

**Thesis statement:** The topic sentence of the topic paragraph. It introduces the subject of an essay.

**Topic sentence:** The first sentence in a paragraph. It introduces the subject that the following sentences will support.

**Topic paragraph:** Consists of a thesis sentence and each topic sentence from the body paragraphs, rewritten in the reverse order of their appearance in the actual essay.

**Validity:** Whether or not an experiment proves what the executor says it proves.

# Index

# Index of Reproducibles